Brad,

Together we
can save the Dream.

You have the power
to inspire others!

D1042278

Louis Hernandez, Jr.

Saving the
American
Dream

main street's last stand

authorHOUSE®

AuthorHouse™
1663 Liberty Drive
Bloomington, IN 47403
www.authorhouse.com
Phone: 1-800-839-8640

Published by AuthorHouse 3/14/2012

ISBN: 978-1-4685-5493-9 (e)
ISBN: 978-1-4685-5494-6 (hc)

Library of Congress Control Number: 2012903135

More Praise ...

"With the passion of someone deeply concerned about local financial institutions and our country, Louis Hernandez, Jr. offers a compelling path toward restoring the economic health and future of our nation." – **Youngme Moon**, *Associate Professor of Business Administration, Harvard Business School*

"The American Dream may be on the critical list but we have time to cure that which ails us. Louis should run for President." – **Juli Anne Callis**, *President and CEO, National Institutes of Health FCU*

"A compelling read for anyone interested in saving the American Dream for this and future generations." – **Brendan McDonough**, Former CEO, HSBC North America

"This book reminded me what the American Dream is and why we need to cherish it. Inspiring." – **Gary Greenfield**, Chairman and CEO, Avid Technology, Inc.

"A skillful presentation of how avarice and faulty governmental programs and approaches contributed greatly to the American Dream not becoming a reality." – **David G. Carter**, Ph.D., Chancellor Emeritus, Connecticut State University System

"Louis Hernandez brings his experience, understanding and passion to a subject important to everyone with an interest in what needs to be done to fix our financial institutions." – **Aron Ain**, CEO, Kronos

"Every high school student in America should read this book. An excellent landscape of the strengths our country has been built on, where and how we lost our way and compelling suggestions for moving forward." – **Weldon "Butch" Leonardson**, *SVP & CIO, BECU, Seattle, WA*

"It is a must-read for anyone proud of this country's history who believes in the importance of preserving our leadership, encouraging competition and stimulating innovation." – **Christine Barry**, *Research Director,* Aite Group

"Louis forcefully calls on political, business and community leaders to pay attention to the crisis and describes what they should do to save Main Street." – **Bill Handel**, *Vice President of Research, Raddon Financial Group*

"I enjoyed traveling through time and feeling Louis' powerful and personal descriptions of how Americans dedicated their lives and souls to achieving the American Dream – and how those opportunities are now at risk." – **Lary B. McCants, CCD, CCE**, *Chairman of the Board, Credit Union Executive Society (CUES)*

"A great read. Informative and relevant for the times. A thoughtful book for Main Street America." – **Mike Watson**, *COO, Capital Community Bank, Provo, UT*

"A wonderful book full of hope. It will spark people to be more committed than ever to achieving their own personal American Dream." – **Prof. Dr. Chira Hongladarom**, *Secretary General, Foundation for International Human Resource Development, Thailand*

"A clear and down-to-earth examination of what is wrong and what needs to be done in America today to revive the right of everyone to pursue the American Dream." – **Guillermo Guemez**, *CIO, Banorte*

"The global impact of this book is undeniable. Written not only for Americans, people from every corner of the world will find it relevant." – **Sittichai Ungphakorn**, *Vice President, Royal Forest Department Savings and Credit Cooperative Limited, Thailand*

"An eye-opening look at how public policy, greed and government programs have gone wrong and spoiled the Dream." – **Steven Post**, *CEO, VSECU, Montpelier, VT*

"Captivating – offers great insight into the critical role 'people oriented' credit unions and banks play in realizing the American Dream." – **Kitty (K) Simons-Wijdenbosch**, *Chief Operations Officer, Coöperatieve Spaar-en Kredietbank GODO G.A., Suriname*

Dedication

I dedicate this book to my family, who created a loving environment full of encouragement, support and a sense of personal accountability. My mother, who worked hard to achieve the American Dream, taught me the value of tireless effort, sacrificing for what you believe in, a strong education and family. My father, a technologist who, like my mother, was also an educator, emphasized enjoying the journey in the pursuit of a better life, committing to what is important and having the courage to do what you think is right. My three sisters taught me the value of working together, collaborating, finding common ground and maintaining an unwavering commitment to family.

My large extended family is a unique example of how different each of us is in our habits, routines and perspectives and yet, despite these differences, how we often share common goals and hopes for a better tomorrow.

Finally, I dedicate this book to my children, who remind me every day why it is so important to preserve the American Dream, carry the torch of inspiration to the rest of the world, and continue to provide the opportunities that draw new citizens to our borders. Our future is in the hands of our children.

Contents

List of Figures

Preface

Two years ago, I published my first book, *Too Small to Fail*, which explored how the fallout from the U.S. financial crisis combined with a host of other circumstances to put at risk one of the most important pillars of American economic strength: the thousands of "Main Street" community banks and credit unions that meet the everyday financial needs of individuals and small businesses in communities nationwide.

In particular, I noted how broad policies that were hastily enacted to curb abuses at some of America's large, capital markets-type banks had created negative unintended consequences for America's smaller, community-based financial institutions. These fiscally conservative and generally well-run small institutions played little role in the subprime mortgage market. They entered the crisis with higher capital and fewer losses than larger banks, but exited much worse off as sweeping policy changes caused them to be punished for the transgressions of their "Too Big to Fail" brethren. More to the point, these unintended consequences put the viability of our smaller financial institutions at risk, along with the communities and small businesses that depend on them.

In the subsequent two years, through conversations with hundreds of business leaders and other people in the U.S. and around the world, I came to realize that it wasn't just community-based financial institutions that were being threatened by the financial crisis and by the rapid changes occurring around the globe. What was being called into question was nothing less than the health and viability of the American Dream.

What really drove the point home for me was the reaction to the U.S. financial crisis by people in other nations across Asia, South America and Europe. In just about every locale I visited, people were genuinely shocked and saddened to see the financial crisis sapping America's spirit and its strength. I understood that, whatever else you might say about America, we had always been a beacon of hope to others, an example of the possibilities for human freedom, equality and prosperity. Our unique blend of democracy and capitalism combined to create opportunities for upward mobility unmatched by any other country or period in history.

As I considered the special place that America held in the global consciousness, I began thinking more and more about the true meaning of the American Dream. Where did it come from? How had it influenced our development as a nation? How did it maintain its relevance throughout our history? What role did this ideal play in justifying the bad policymaking, greed and overindulgence that culminated in the financial crisis? And what can be done to restore the American Dream and make it relevant once again?

I believe that the near-collapse of financial systems we have seen in the U.S., Europe and elsewhere was not the cause, but rather the symptom of a larger breakdown in the social order resulting from a series of rapid changes taking place in the world today. In the U.S., it is a combination of external forces (increasing economic and social globalism; the U.S. shift from a manufacturing to a knowledge economy; the widespread adoption of advanced computer and communications technologies) and internal forces (monetary and economic policies; public attitudes, values and expectations; changing educational, workforce and income demographics; and shifts in consumer behavior) that have led to the breakdown not only of major financial systems, but to a gradual erosion of the American Dream.

It is instructive to view these changes in their historical perspective, as each new circumstance brought about important changes in policy and public attitudes. That is why I have devoted considerable attention to the economic and political evolution of the American Dream, to show how these changes built upon one another to produce our current predicament. As we come to terms with these changes, I am hopeful that we will be able to recalibrate outdated expectations, reverse unsuccessful policies, and refocus our energies toward creating a sustainable social contract and a stronger, more responsive financial system.

Banking has played a central role in the narrative of American history, and it likewise plays a central role in the narrative of this book. Without credit and the economic stimulus it provides, there would have been no industrial or technology revolutions, no business creation, no jobs, no prosperity and no innovation. It is my belief that one of the most important tasks we face in the coming years is to fully restore the health of our financial institutions – large and small – before we can address the other changes needed to prosper in the 21st century.

The recent implosion of our financial system was the culmination of events that had been years in the making. It was a "perfect storm" of public policy, an entitlement culture and just plain greed that made it possible for a few large institutions to set off the most damaging economic catastrophe in our working lives and erode the public trust in financial institutions of all kinds.

Our government's response to the financial crisis to date has been a series of policies that seek to de-risk banking, stabilize the economy and protect the consumer. Unfortunately, in de-risking the banking system, we have made it harder for all banks to issue loans and continue supporting the American Dream. While larger banks have been able to make up for reduced lending through other sources of income – such as insurance, stock trading, investment banking and hedge fund operations – our nation's smaller banks and credit unions continue to suffer because they have no such options. The result is the economy and jobs have been undermined, consumers are worse off, and our community-based financial institutions are unjustly being punished. I believe that resolving this basic injustice remains one of the first steps we must take to restore the financial system's overall health.

It is my hope that readers of this book will gain a better appreciation of the significant challenges that America faces today; recognize the policies, circumstances and attitudes that shaped our present situation; understand the global realities to which we must adapt; and commit themselves to making the changes needed to restore the fundamental tenets of the American Dream.

As an entrepreneur who has been involved in setting economic policy and as a veteran of the financial services industry for many years, I have personally witnessed the growing disconnect between Wall Street and Main Street, and I have been a vocal critic of policies aimed at Wall Street that end up hurting Main Street financial institutions. Every day, I realize how important our Main Street institutions are to the American Dream – a dream that I myself have always believed in and pursued. We have a great many cultural, economic and educational advantages in this country that we cannot afford to lose. Something must be done to save our American Dream, and it must be done now.

Louis Hernandez, Jr.

Acknowledgements

Many people were involved in bringing this book to life, and I am deeply indebted to all of them for their advice, assistance and patience.

I particularly appreciate the support and insights I received from my many friends in the community bank and credit union industry, and the staff of Open Solutions, who made it possible to manage the demands of writing alongside the demands of running a software company.

I must also acknowledge the efforts of my editorial team – Dan McGowan, Lizette Nigro, Brad Scholz, Peter Weiland, Pat Bator and Staasi Heropoulos – who researched many of the topics in this book, and tirelessly reviewed and edited the manuscript. Brad, in particular, devoted much time and effort toward making this a polished work of prose, while Lizette and Dan kept the project on track.

I'd like to extend my thanks to Bill Handel, Vice President of Research at the Raddon Financial Group, for contributing a large amount of original research to this book, including his insightful essays on Fannie Mae and TARP. Bill and the rest of the team at Raddon are among the most clear-eyed analysts of the financial services industry I know.

The leaders of some of the nation's finest community banks and credit unions – and the individuals who have worked with them – were also kind enough to share their personal reflections on the unique role that community-based financial institutions play in supporting the American Dream. For sharing their stories, which appear throughout the book, I would like to thank: Carrie Birkhofer, President and CEO, Bay Federal Credit Union; Milagros Brathwaite, Owner, Brathwaite Transportation, Inc.; Juli Anne Callis, President and CEO, National Institutes of Health Federal Credit Union; Bruce Ingraham, President, Beacon Credit Union; Harley Jacobs, President, Capital Community Bank; Frank Keating, President and CEO, American Bankers Association; Lary B. McCants (CCD, CCE), Chairman, Credit Union Executives Society; Joseph Newberry, President and CEO, Redstone Federal Credit Union; Gary Oakland, President and CEO, Boeing Employees Credit Union; Joan Opp, President and CEO, Stanford Federal Credit Union; Steven Post, CEO, VSECU; Kazik Skoczylas, former banking executive; and Noah W. Wilcox, President and CEO, Grand Rapids State Bank.

I asked several friends and associates whose opinions I respect to read this book and offer their feedback. In addition to those listed above for contributing their stories to the book, I am grateful to the following people for taking time to carefully review the manuscript and provide their considered thoughts and suggestions: Aron Ain, CEO, Kronos; Christine Barry, Research Director, Aite Group; David G. Carter, Ph.D., Chancellor Emeritus, Connecticut State University System and President Emeritus, Eastern Connecticut State University; Dr. Elizabeth M. Daley, Dean, USC School of Cinema/Television; Dennis Dollar, Former Chairman, National Credit Union Administration (NCUA); Mark Greene, CEO, FICO; Gary Greenfield, Chairman and CEO, Avid Technology, Inc.; Guillermo Guemez, CIO, Banorte; Prof. Dr. Chira Hongladarom, Secretary General, Foundation for International Human Resource Development, Thailand; Weldon "Butch" Leonardson, SVP & CIO, BECU; Eng Hong Lim, Partner & ASEAN Practise Leader, Ernst & Young LLP, Singapore; Lary B. McCants, CCD, CCE Chairman of the Board, Credit Union Executive Society (CUES); Brendan McDonough, Former CEO, HSBC North America; Youngme Moon, Associate Professor of Business Administration, Harvard

Business School; Frank Netto, Senior Video Project Specialist, Yankee Candle Company; Bruce Philp, Author, *Consumer Republic*; Steve Potisk, Broadcast Correspondent, Marketwatch.com; Craig Rydin, Former President and CEO, Yankee Candle Company; Robert Scholz, Partner, Evans, Scholz, Williams and Warncke, Atlanta; Kitty Simons-Wijdenbosch, Chief Operations Officer, Coöperatieve Spaar-en Kredietbank GODO G.A., Suriname; Sittichai Ungphakorn, Vice President, Royal Forest Department Savings and Credit Cooperative Limited, Thailand; Mike Watson, COO/CIO, Capital Community Bank; and David Weidner, *The Wall Street Journal.*

For managing my schedule – which is a full-time job in itself – and the countless particulars that go into planning, writing, editing and producing a book, I would like to thank my talented and valued assistants, Sarah Buonfiglio and Kira Rivera.

There are many other people to whom I need to extend thanks for ideas, feedback, research, fact-checking, copyediting, proofreading, design, production, publicity and promotion. You know who you are, and I deeply appreciate the contribution that each of you has made.

1: What is the American Dream?

"The United States is unique because
we are an empire of ideals." [1]

Ronald Reagan

On a recent business trip to the Philippines, I found myself with a few hours to spare and decided to visit the Port district of Manila. I was involved in a sideline photography project at the time, and thought the area might provide some interesting subjects.

When I arrived, I wandered into the neighborhood of Parola, Tondo, one of the vast slums surrounding the port. These slums are makeshift cities, piled up alongside a polluted river below the street. There is no electricity, no clean water, no sewage system, and the moist air along the river is saturated with a tenacious, pungent stench. The slums are a dense junkyard of ramshackle, three-story shanties, hastily erected from rusting sheets of corrugated steel, scrap plywood and other second-hand materials.

As I wandered three levels down among these rickety homes, I spotted several people crouching together in a small room. The room was barely large enough to contain their bodies, and the structure above them appeared so weak that I thought it might collapse at any moment. Inside, I noticed one teenager wearing a t-shirt with a Nike swoosh logo and bright red Nike running shoes. The girl next to him was wearing a pair of True Religion jeans – undoubtedly knock-offs that she purchased for a few hundred pesos on the streets of Manila.

---

[1] Ronald Reagan, Speech to the Republican National Convention, Houston, TX, August 17, 1992.

Meanwhile, an older kid, probably in his early twenties, had on a faded green Polo shirt with the unmistakable horseman and mallet insignia.

I remember thinking that these kids could easily get up, wash their faces off and go three levels up to the street and, if you didn't know where they had just come from, you would think they were a group of young people from an upper middle-class American home. Their clothes displayed all the proper symbols of American affluence and success, the cultural icons of the American Dream.

The American Dream is a powerful notion that has enchanted people from all corners of the globe for hundreds of years. Many who can afford the passage come to our country to try and achieve it. Those who can't, like the residents of the Manila slums I visited, live it by proxy: through the logo-bearing clothes they wear, the popular American music they listen to, and the Hollywood movies and television shows that fill their screens.

From near and far, people throughout the world envy and want the things we have here in America – the freedom, the money, and the opportunity to live a good and fulfilling life. Other nations, too, admire what America has achieved. In many cases, they have strived to reproduce – or even improve upon – the economic and social vitality that lie at the heart of the American Dream. It is a dream that we have fought to preserve and protect for nearly 250 years – economically, legislatively and, when necessary, militarily.

The freedom to pursue what we want, at the rate we want, defines the American character. The ability to pursue any business ambition our abilities and effort will sustain, any educational level our intelligence will support, and any material comforts our incomes will allow, creates an energy that drives our economic productivity and our spiritual strength.

The American Dream is a remarkable idea. I have personally benefited from it, and I'm sure many of you have, as well. Our society and its ideals have made it possible for me to get the education I wanted, to have a wonderful home and family, to pursue my ambitions in business – participating in the founding of numerous entrepreneurial ventures, serving on the boards of several large corporations, and becoming the head of a global software company – and still have time and energy left to devote to charitable causes and helping others.

I have also been fortunate enough to have a say in how our country is run, which is a fundamental American principle. Throughout the years, I have worked with business and political leaders to help shape economic, technology and education policy at the state and national levels, serving as chair of the Connecticut Technology Council, and vice-chair of the Connecticut Governor's Council on Economic Competitiveness and Technology, and in other executive policymaking positions.

It is precisely because I deeply value the American Dream that it troubles and concerns me to see this dream being threatened today by the disproportionate influence of corporations and special interest groups, poorly thought-out government policies, and an erosion of the American values of financial prudence and hard work. In particular, I am troubled by the actions taken to save our largest banks in the wake of the financial crisis that unfairly punished many smaller community banks and credit unions that played little or no role in the crisis.

I believe that multiple components of the American Dream – including our model of employment, home ownership, business formation and wealth accumulation – are at risk this very moment because of a fundamental disconnect between our public policy and the conditions needed to achieve this dream. In the name of consumer protection, economic stability and financial safety and soundness, our policymakers and those who influence them have undermined the very tenets of this dream.

Before we examine how it was possible for the American Dream to get into the mess it's in today, it is useful to appreciate the enduring ideals it represents...to remind ourselves how the dream came to be, how it drew others to our country, how its meaning has evolved over time and, finally, how it has been exported to other parts of the world. In later chapters, we shall also explore how the unrestrained pursuit of the American Dream – fueled by profits, policy, and a prevailing sense of entitlement – may hold the very seeds of the dream's destruction.

Origins of the American Dream

By most accounts, the phrase "the American Dream" was coined by a popular U.S. historian named James Truslow Adams. In his 1931 book, *Epic of America*, he referred to it as the "dream of a land in which life should be better and richer and fuller for every man, with opportunity for each according to ability or achievement," adding, "It is not a dream of motor cars and high wages merely, but a dream of social order in which each man and each woman shall be able to attain to the fullest stature of which they are innately capable, and be recognized by others for what they are, regardless of the fortuitous circumstances of birth or position." [2]

This idyllic vision of universal upward mobility was undoubtedly a welcome one considering that America was, at the time, suffering through one of the most staggering financial calamities ever: the Great Depression, when the stock market lost 30% of its value, approximately ten thousand banks failed, industrial production was

---

[2] James Truslow Adams, *The Epic of America* (Boston: Little, Brown and Co., 1931) 214-215.

cut nearly in half, Gross Domestic Product (GDP) declined by 30%, and one in four Americans was out of work.

While Adams may have popularized the idea of the American Dream, he certainly didn't invent it. Adams was, in fact, mostly restating ideas and principles that originated with America's founding fathers, and that remained intact throughout numerous wars, social upheavals and economic setbacks.

Almost every American school child understands the core idea underlying the American Dream. It is right in front of them when they recite the second sentence of the Declaration of Independence, which reads: "We hold these truths to be self-evident, that all men are created equal, that they are endowed by their Creator with certain unalienable Rights, that among these are Life, Liberty and the pursuit of Happiness."

Equality and the pursuit of happiness. To most of us, these are what the dream is all about – even if the specific components of "happiness" change with each cultural shift and each new generation to enter American society.

These are also the qualities that have made America unique. In a world beset by class distinctions, oppressive government regimes, religious discrimination and limited economic possibilities, our nation has always been a land of opportunity. In America, the belief goes, talent and ambition will trump race, religion, nationality, class and just about any other potentially limiting social characteristic. In America, the new immigrant and the common man are free to succeed.

Immigration and the American Dream

Alexis de Tocqueville, a French nobleman and political scientist deeply enamored with the ideals and promise of the United States, traveled to the U.S. during the 1830s to study our young nation. He recorded his impressions in the landmark book, *Democracy in America* – still one of the most discerning appraisals of the uniquely American way of life. In that book, he referred to the American Dream as "the charm of anticipated success."[3]

Of course, de Tocqueville was neither the first nor the last foreign citizen to be seduced by this charm. In fact, America has always been a land of foreigners and a land of opportunity. For more than 275 years, people from virtually every country in the world have been drawn to our shores with the same anticipation of success as our own population, whether that "success" meant freedom, education, property ownership, employment opportunities, or financial security.

In 2009, the most recent year for which data is available, there were approximately 307,000,000 people in the U.S., and slightly more than 12% of this total (roughly 38,500,000) was immigrants.[4] Over the next few years, census officials expect the U.S. population to grow by about 2.8 million individuals per year, with 40% of this growth coming from immigration.[5]

In fact, almost everyone in America is the descendant of an immigrant who came here to pursue a dream, including me. Both of my parents are of Spanish ancestry. My father grew up in a blue-collar neighborhood outside of Detroit, Michigan. My grandfather supported my grandmother and their five children by working as

---

[3]   Alexis De Tocqueville, *Democracy in America Volume 3* (London: Saunders and Otley, 1840) 147.
[4]   U.S. Census Bureau, 2009 American Community Survey.
[5]   U.S. Census Bureau, 2009 National Population Projections, Low Net International Migration Series.

a laborer in a manufacturing plant for over 45 years. The children enjoyed the benefits of America's culture and educational system during their youth. Like so many immigrants, my father later served his country in the armed forces, used the GI Bill to receive an extensive university education, and became a technologist and educator. My mother came to America as a teenager, with very little education. Through hard work, studying, and taking advantage of the opportunities that were afforded to her, she worked her way through college, earned a Ph.D., and became a director of a large school district in northern California following a long career as an educator. All of this, clearly, represented a long journey from the small village in Mexico where she was raised.

As my own story illustrates, America is truly a melting pot, with a large and steady influx of naturalized citizens who enrich and redefine the national character, influence our economy, and occasionally challenge our social infrastructure.

Historians generally cite four major waves of immigration that had a major impact on the U.S., and consequently on shaping the American Dream. The first wave took place in colonial times, roughly from the late 1600s to the late 1700s. This is when the first English and European settlers came to America seeking to make their living off of our abundant farmland. Toward the end of this wave, the colonies even offered inducements to encourage additional immigration. The so-called "headright system," adopted by Virginia and other early colonies during the mid-1700s, granted 50 acres of land to any Englishman who could afford to pay for his Atlantic crossing, and an additional 50 acres to each of his sons and servants.

Notable American Immigrant Business Leaders:

- **Sergey Brin**, cofounder of Google (Russia)
- **Roberto Críspulo Goizueta**, former chairman and CEO of Coca-Cola (Cuba)
- **Liz Claiborne**, fashion designer (Belgium)
- **Charles Wang**, founder of Computer Associates (China)
- **Indra Nooyi**, CEO of PepsiCo (India)
- **Andy Grove**, cofounder of Intel (Hungary)
- **Kevork S. Hovnanian**, home builder, founder of Hovnanian Enterprises (Iraq)
- **Jerry Yang**, cofounder of Yahoo! (Japan)
- **Andrew Carnegie**, Steel magnate and philanthropist (Scotland)
- **Levi Strauss**, clothing maker (Germany)

The second large wave of immigration occurred roughly from 1820 until the mid-1870s, when approximately 8.5 million people – mostly German, Irish and Italian – immigrated to the U.S. Many of these immigrants were also seeking land on which to farm and raise their families, as well as to escape harsh conditions in their native lands, notably the potato famine that was affecting Ireland. By the time this second wave ended, its immigrants represented nearly 25% of the total U.S. population, which was estimated at 38.5 million.[6]

During the third major immigration wave, between 1881 and 1920, approximately 23 million more people arrived in the U.S., largely from northern, eastern and southern Europe, but also from China.[7] This group was seeking the abundant employment opportunities and higher pay that were available in America. Many of the immigrants of

---

[6]   Department of Homeland Security, "Persons Obtaining Legal Permanent Resident Status: Fiscal Years 1820 to 2010," *Yearbook of Immigration Statistics*, 2011.

[7]   Ibid.

this period would have arrived by ship into New York harbor, sailing past the Statue of Liberty and its welcoming inscription: "Give me your tired, your poor, your huddled masses yearning to breathe free." No wonder they believed in the American Dream!

U.S. immigration slowed for a period after the 1920s, partly because America was having trouble digesting its many new citizens. Social tensions had been slowly mounting among various immigrant groups, as well as between immigrants and America's more established citizens. Seeking to contain the problem, Congress passed the Emergency Quota Act and the Immigration Act of 1924, which limited the number of newcomers that would be permitted in the U.S. from various countries.

Another reason immigration temporarily slowed was the Great Depression of the 1930s. For the first time, a shadow had been cast upon the American Dream and the unlimited economic prospects that America seemed to offer. This may be why, during the 1930s, more people emigrated from the United States than immigrated to it.

The latest wave of immigration began in the mid-1960s and has continued into the 21st century. Among the catalysts for this wave of immigration were the passage of the Immigration and Nationality Act of 1965 and the later Immigration Act of 1990, which abolished the national-origin quotas enacted during previous decades.

More than 33 million newcomers became U.S. citizens between 1965 and 2010, and the composition of this wave was markedly different from earlier waves. About half of the current wave of immigrants comes from Mexico and Latin America, about a quarter comes from Asian countries, and only about a fifth comes from Europe.[8]

---

[8] Ibid.

A Uniquely American Success Story

Immigrants have always left a large footprint on American culture and American business. Amadeo Giannini, founder of Bank of America, made one of the bigger footprints.

The son of Italian immigrant parents, Giannini established the Bank of Italy in San Francisco in 1904 to serve the needs of fellow immigrants and other people – primarily from the lower rungs of the socio-economic ladder – that larger banks were refusing to serve. With considerable business savvy, Giannini managed to parlay his success with the Bank of Italy (which grew to 101 branches) into a series of ever-larger bank acquisitions and mergers, culminating in a 1928 merger with Bank of America Los Angeles. The resulting institution became the foundation for what is today the largest bank in America by assets, and a global financial services powerhouse.

Part of Giannini's success came from a fortuitous move he made after the 1906 earthquake in San Francisco. Shortly after the earthquake struck, Giannini removed all the cash from his vaults and transported it, via garbage wagon, to the nearby town of San Mateo. Other bankers, who did not share Giannini's foresight, left their funds in vaults that, because of the fires that swept through San Francisco after the earthquake, could not be opened for weeks without risking damage to the money inside.

As a result of this well-timed decision, Giannini was one of the very few bankers equipped to provide loans after the earthquake. He reportedly ran his "bank" from a plank resting across two barrels in the street and made loans, secured by little more than a handshake, to people who needed money to rebuild what the quake had destroyed. Those who knew him say Giannini took pride in the fact that every single one of the loans he made during this time was repaid.

In a 1998 speech, former President Bill Clinton praised America's history of immigration. "The United States has always been energized by its immigrant populations," he stated, adding, "They have proved to be the most restless, the most adventurous, the most innovative, and the most industrious of people."[9]

Commenting more recently on the importance of a healthy immigrant population, Clinton suggested that immigration would become increasingly essential to grow the U.S. economy, counter the effects of an aging population, and provide support for the long-term finances of Medicare and Social Security.[10]

Lady Liberty: A Promise of Opportunity...

I arrived in America from England in 1953 as a nine-year-old boy and everything I knew about this country came from comic books and movies. I expected to see gangsters and cowboys in the streets. But the scene that welcomed my family to America after a six-day Atlantic voyage was Lady Liberty and her promise of opportunity. Thinking about it today still chokes me up.

I was excited to be coming to a new country. Our family was unable to return to my father's native Poland after World War II because of the Communist occupation, so we came to America to pursue our dreams, moving into an ethnic, working class neighborhood in East Hartford, CT. My father said America was a great place, a land where hard work is rewarded and optimism is validated.

(continued on next page)

---

[9] Bill Clinton, Commencement Address, Portland State University, Portland, OR, June 13, 1998.

[10] Bill Clinton, Peter G Peterson Foundation 2010 Fiscal Summit, Washington, DC, April 28, 2010.

When I was 15, my father died of a heart attack. As the eldest of three children, I worked to support our family. I had three paper routes and worked as a part-time landscaper during high school. I knew higher education was a path to success, but college was not an expense my family could afford. So I joined the Air Force as a radio operator. I learned Morse code and became proficient at typing the messages I decrypted. Little did I know my typing ability would lead to my first civilian job – a position in the mortgage department at Hartford National Bank.

I spent most of my career working for banks and credit unions. Through dedication and hard work I assumed several executive-level banking positions. My wife and I adopted a baby girl, raising her in the home we owned near Hartford. We lived a comfortable life and wanted for nothing. America had proven to be the land of opportunity, as promised.

Today, I am happy and content in retirement, and I have lived the American Dream. My life didn't follow the path I envisioned as a boy, but I learned that when something is missing, you find another path. America gave me chances and choices.

On Lady Liberty's 100th anniversary in America, I raised money for the Statue of Liberty Restoration Fund. It was important for me to do this. As an immigrant, I wanted to make sure this symbol of American promise and opportunity would always be there to inspire somebody else, the way she inspired me.

Kazik Skoczylas, Former Bank Executive
Connecticut

It is clear that understanding the changing composition of the American population and finding ways to productively address the current wave of immigration has important implications for the economy, for financial institutions, and for the American Dream as a whole.

Changing Views of the American Dream

Ever since the phrase entered popular discourse, virtually every political, business and religious leader has used the American Dream to define and set the standard for our nation's progress and direction. Some leaders embodied the principles of the American Dream before the concept itself was fully formed. Benjamin Franklin and Abraham Lincoln come immediately to mind. Other leaders, of more recent vintage, who embody the American Dream include Dr. Martin Luther King, Jr., Barack Obama and Warren Buffet. What each of these men has in common is that they started from relatively humble beginnings and, through their own talents and efforts, rose to the very heights of influence, power and success.

Like other grand concepts, the meaning of the American Dream has been subject to constant reinterpretation and change. So, it is not surprising to find that different leaders have expressed different understandings of what the dream is about, and what they think it should mean to us. To some, the American Dream is about education. To others, it is about economic freedom…or equality…or owning a home…or forming a business.

Barack Obama, in a 2007 campaign speech, considered the American Dream to be one of simple aspirations:

> *In big cities and small towns; among men and women; young and old; black, white, and brown – Americans share a faith in simple dreams. A job with wages that can support a family.*

Health care that we can count on and afford. A retirement that is dignified and secure. Education and opportunity for our kids. Common hopes. American dreams.[11]

Nearly 50 years earlier, Dr. Martin Luther King, Jr., had a very different understanding of the American Dream, reflecting the racial discrimination and inequality that prevailed at the time, which prevented many citizens from achieving the dream. The dream he envisioned in his historic August 1963 speech during the March on Washington, was not concerned with everyday matters, but with the overall direction of American society.

And so even though we face the difficulties of today and to-morrow, I still have a dream. It is a dream deeply rooted in the American dream.

I have a dream that one day this nation will rise up and live out the true meaning of its creed: "We hold these truths to be self-evident, that all men are created equal.

I have a dream that one day on the red hills of Georgia, the sons of former slaves and the sons of former slave owners will be able to sit down together at the table of brotherhood.

I have a dream that one day even the state of Mississippi, a state sweltering with the heat of injustice, sweltering with the heat of oppression, will be transformed into an oasis of freedom and justice.

I have a dream that my four little children will one day live in a nation where they will not be judged by the color of their skin but by the content of their character.[12]

[11] Barack Obama, Campaign Speech, Bettendorf, IA, November 7, 2007.
[12] Rev. Dr. Martin Luther King, Jr., "I Have a Dream" Speech, Washington, DC, August 28, 1963.

For George H.W. Bush, the American Dream meant not just doing something for yourself, but also doing for others:

> *The American Dream means giving it your all, trying your hardest, accomplishing something. And then I'd add to that, giving something back. No definition of a successful life can do anything but include serving others.*[13]

For Bill Clinton, the American Dream was about the power of our common bonds:

> *We need a spirit of community, a sense that we are all in this together. If we have no sense of community, the American dream will wither.*[14]

To the second George Bush, the American Dream was about equality and diversity:

> *I have faith that with God's help we as a nation will move forward together as one nation, indivisible. And together we will create an America that is open, so every citizen has access to the American dream; an America that is educated, so every child has the keys to realize that dream; and an America that is united in our diversity and our shared American values that are larger than race or party.*[15]

For Herbert Hoover (who notoriously failed to deliver on the promise), the American Dream meant, simply:

> *A chicken in every pot. A car in every garage.*[16]

---

[13] George H.W. Bush, Academy of Achievement Interview, June 2, 1995.
[14] Bill Clinton, Announcement Speech, Little Rock, AR, October 2, 1991.
[15] George W. Bush, Acceptance Speech, Austin, TX, December 13, 2000.
[16] Republican Party Campaign Ad, *New York Times*, October 30, 1928.

And for Franklin Delano Roosevelt, the American Dream was about being realistic and prudent in one's expectations about the dream itself:

> *In the older days a great financial fortune was too often the goal. To rule through wealth, or through the power of wealth, fired our imagination. This was the dream of the gold ladder –each individual for himself.*
>
> *It is my firm belief that the newer generation of America has a different dream. You place emphasis on sufficiency of life, rather than on a plethora of riches. You think of the security for yourself and your family that will give you good health, good food, good education, good working conditions, and the opportunity for normal recreation and occasional travel. Your advancement, your hope is along a broad highway on which thousands of your fellow men and women are advancing with you.*[17]

If these examples show us anything, it is that the American Dream remains a dynamic and malleable idea. This is not necessarily a bad thing. It simply underscores the power inherent in the idea, in the same way that the U.S. Constitution subjects itself to – and survives – constant challenges, questioning and interpretations.

In a famous 1964 Supreme Court case, Justice Potter Stewart was asked to decide whether or not a movie called *The Lovers* should be labeled "hard-core pornography." After thinking long and hard about the nuances of the problem, the Justice finally stated: "I shall not today attempt further to define the kinds of material I understand to be embraced within that shorthand description; and perhaps I could never succeed in intelligibly doing so. But I know it when I see it."[18]

---

[17] Franklin D. Roosevelt, Radio Address to the Young Democratic Clubs of America, August 24, 1935.

[18] Justice Potter Stewart, Concurring Opinion, Jacobellis v. Ohio, 378 U.S. 184 (1964).

So, perhaps that's how it is with the American Dream. Even as we constantly struggle to define it, we know it when we see it.

Exporting the American Dream

Numerous technologies that were developed and perfected over the past 100 years have made the world a global village. Radio and television have made it possible to transmit spoken words and moving images almost instantly across long distances. Film and video technologies have made it possible to record, preserve and share events and performances worldwide. Affordable air transportation has enabled people to travel at will to practically any locale in the world. The transistor, the microchip and digital storage technologies have allowed people to access, process and transmit huge amounts of information using ever-faster, cheaper and more powerful computers. Mobile phones, the World Wide Web and the Internet – which have penetrated some of the most remote parts of the world – have given citizens of every country the power to communicate and share information in real-time.

To appreciate how much our world has changed, just think about the role that social networking technologies like Facebook, Twitter and YouTube (innovations that were all created in America) played in mobilizing the 2011 uprisings in the Middle East. Consider how Egypt attempted to avert an uprising within its own borders by blocking access to the nation's Internet and cell phone networks. Think about how the U.S. scored several years' worth of intelligence data simply by snatching Osama Bin Laden's hard disk.

It's not just information that crosses borders effortlessly today. Significantly, it's also culture and ideas. And, despite what other countries may think of our politics and our military presence, no culture has spread so widely throughout the world or so thoroughly

Louis Hernandez, Jr.

dominated global entertainment venues as American popular culture.

Just like the kids in the Philippines slums who express their admiration for American culture with their blue jeans and branded attire, you see American movies playing in theaters from Singapore to Budapest. James Cameron's blockbuster movie, Avatar, has been distributed in 64 different countries, translated into dozens of languages, and become the top-grossing film of all time, earning more than $2 billion worldwide.[19] American cinema also inspired film production overseas. Notably, it gave rise to the Hindi-language "Bollywood" film industry in India (which has now surpassed Hollywood to become the world's largest film producer).

American popular music is often heard on radio stations and iPod playlists in many corners of the world, and localized versions of American musical trends influence the best-selling music in many countries. In fact, half of the top ten best selling albums of all time worldwide were recorded by American artists.[20]

Likewise, American television shows, books and magazines are distributed and translated around the world, playing the role of cultural emissaries for the American way of life.

What makes this significant is that the exportation of American popular culture is really about the exportation of American middle-class values that are central to the American Dream. The world is perennially fascinated by our uniquely democratic, capitalist system, and the products, ideas and opportunities it produces. The advent of new technologies like digital music players, e-book readers and

[19] "All Time Box Office Worldwide Grosses," *Box Office Mojo*, November 2011, http://www.boxofficemojo.com/alltime/world/.

[20] Wikipedia Contributors, "List of Best-Selling Albums," *Wikipedia, The Free Encyclopedia*, November 2011, http://en.wikipedia.org/wiki/List of best-selling albums worldwide.

smart phones has only accelerated the breadth and speed with which American culture is able to reach people in other societies.

America's cultural influence extends beyond entertainment, of course. Our educational and political systems have also had a tremendous impact on other nations. Our manufacturing and business practices have been studied and emulated by emerging and established industrial economies, just as we borrowed numerous ideas from Japanese manufacturers. Today, many of our largest corporations generate significantly more revenue from international sales than domestic sales, and maintain offices in nearly every major city in the world.

For instance, Coca-Cola is available in practically every country in the world and sold on every continent except Antarctica. McDonalds, whose golden arches are more recognizable than the Christian cross, serves its food in more than 120 countries – often with menus tailored specifically to local tastes. [21]

The English language is spoken and understood in more countries than any other language, and is the most popular second language in schools around the world.[22] American business, scientific and technological innovations are routinely shared with the worldwide community through global research and academic organizations. Even the Internet, the most powerful tool ever developed for globalization, was largely an American invention, originating at the U.S. Department of Defense.

While other countries and cultures may seem impenetrable to Americans, it is fair to say that our own culture is exceptionally well studied, well disseminated and well understood. Because of this,

---

[21] Sponsorship Research International, *The Golden Arches*, 1995.
[22] M. Paul Lewis, ed., *Ethnologue: 16th Edition* (Dallas, TX: SIL International Publications, 2009).

many other countries desire not only to emulate various components of the American Dream, but also to invest in them.

Aggregate Foreign Investment

The American Dream has been a major force behind the strength of the U.S. economy. And the strength of the U.S. economy has, in turn, been responsible for attracting considerable foreign investment. Foreign-owned assets in the U.S. grew rapidly over most of the past 30 years (dropping dramatically only in response to the subprime mortgage crisis), as shown in Figure 1.

Figure 1 - Foreign Owned Assets in the U.S., 1980-2010
($ Trillions)

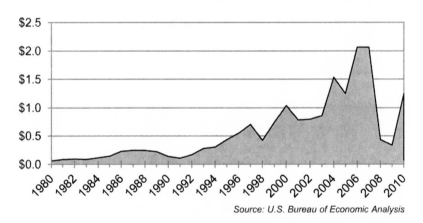

Source: U.S. Bureau of Economic Analysis

In addition to direct foreign investment in U.S. assets, foreign banks and investors own a huge share of consumer and mortgage debt, largely through derivatives such as CDOs, CMOs and other structured investment vehicles.

Foreign Real Estate Investment

America is by far the most popular country in the world for foreign real estate purchases, accounting for nearly 43% of all acquisitions in 2010, more than twice the amount of the runner-up United Kingdom.[23] Although much of this represents commercial real estate transactions, a sizable number represents home transactions. According to the National Association of Realtors, foreign nationals, recent immigrants, and individuals with long-term visas accounted for approximately $81 billion worth of existing homes sales in 2011 and nearly 62% of these purchases were all cash, with no mortgage financing.[24]

Foreign Investment in U.S. Auto Industry

Foreign companies know that Americans love their cars. So much so that there are now nine foreign-based automobile companies producing vehicles in fifteen auto plants in the United States. According to a 2007 report by the Department of Commerce, these manufacturers have total investments valued at over $66 billion in the United States, with $44.7 billion specifically from motor vehicle producers.[25]

What's more, foreign-owned manufacturers are beating us at our own game. As the next chart shows, foreign-owned light vehicle production increased at a compound annual growth rate (CAGR) of 10.7% between 1986 and 2007, while production by Detroit's "Big Three" automakers declined at a CAGR of 0.2% during the same period.[26]

---

[23] Association of Foreign Investors in Real Estate, *2011 AFIRE Annual Survey*, 2011.

[24] Lawrence Yun, et al., *Profile of International Home Buying Activity 2011_* (Washington, DC: National Association of Realtors, May 2011).

[25] Office of Aerospace and Automotive Industries, International Trade Association, *Foreign-Based Companies Investing in the U.S. Auto Industry* (Washington, DC: U.S. Dept. of Commerce, August 2007).

[26] Ibid.

Figure 2 - U.S. Light Vehicle Production, 1986-2007
(Millions)

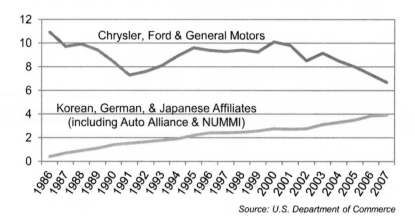

Source: U.S. Department of Commerce

Foreign Investment in the Movie Industry

OK, I admit that this is not a major economic indicator. But since I mentioned earlier how Hollywood movies played a starring role in spreading American culture around the globe, I wanted to note that even the movie industry is influenced by foreign investment. In fact, three of the America's seven major film distributors – Sony, Universal and Fox – are not actually American companies. They are owned by parent companies based in Japan, Canada and Australia, respectively.

Foreign Enrollment in U.S. Colleges and Universities

The composition of American colleges and universities has also been dramatically affected by the exportation of the American Dream. Foreign enrollment in U.S. institutions of higher education has grown steadily from the mid 1950s until today, increasing nearly 2,000% to reach 723,277 international students that are now enrolled in U.S. colleges and universities.[27]

---

[27] P. Chow and R. Bhandari, *2010 Open Doors Report on International Educational Exchange*, (New York: Institute of International Education, 2010).

Figure 3 - Foreign Students in U.S. Colleges and Universities, 1950-2010

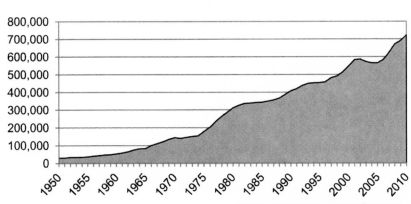

Source: Institute of International Education

Also worth noting is the fact that students from just three countries – China, India and South Korea – made up 44% of all international students studying in the U.S. in 2010.[28]

Foreign Investment in U.S. National Debt

Perhaps the most significant way that other countries around the world invest in the American Dream is by buying our debt. And there's lots of it to go around…more than $15 trillion worth at the end of 2011.[29] Despite recent turmoil in our financial markets and last-minute negotiations to increase the U.S. debt ceiling, U.S. Treasuries are still considered one of the safest investments in the world.

According to 2011 figures from the U.S. Treasury, China is the largest foreign owner of America's debt, holding $1.15 trillion (7.7%) of it.

---

[28] Ibid.
[29] U.S. Dept. of Treasury, *Monthly Statement of the Public Debt of the United States*, December 31, 2011.

Japan comes next, holding $956.8 billion (6.4%). These two countries are followed by:[30]

- United Kingdom ($421.6 billion = 2.8%)

- OPEC countries ($229.9 billion = 1.5%)

- Brazil ($206.2 billion = 1.4%)

- Caribbean Banking Centers ($173.0 billion = 1.2%)

- Taiwan ($149.3 billion = 1.0%)

- Switzerland ($146.1 billion = 0.9%)

While it makes interesting dinner conversation to complain that foreign countries "own America," the truth is that America itself owns the largest share of its debt, primarily through holdings of the Social Security Trust Fund, the U.S. Treasury, U.S. households, and state and local governments.

The reason I have detailed the various ways that other nations are investing in the American Dream is not to suggest that we should fear their investment, but to highlight the degree of economic and cultural interconnectivity that exists among world economies today. Like the ever-widening ripple that grows from a raindrop falling into still water, events – both economic and political – that originate in one place now quickly spread to others. This is apparent by looking at the global economic impact of such recent events as the tsunami in Japan, the Greek debt crisis, the political upheaval in the Middle East, and the U.S. sub-prime mortgage debacle.

---

[30] U.S. Dept. of Treasury, *Major Foreign Holders of Treasury Securities*, November 16, 2011.

2: Tenets of the American Dream

"One true measure of a nation is its success in fulfilling the promise of a better life for each of its members. Let this be the measure of our nation." [31]
John F. Kennedy

While the basic tenets of the American Dream have remained fairly constant (equality, freedom, the opportunity to improve one's situation in life and fulfill one's potential), the societal focus of these tenets has changed dramatically over time. For example, from today's vantage point – with our concerns about Wall Street booms and busts, declining real estate prices and frozen credit markets – it's easy to forget that the epitome of the American Dream for most of our nation's history centered not on having your own home, but on having your own farm.

In colonial times, 90% of the American population was involved in farming in one form or another. During the mid-1800s, hordes of Americans, largely of European descent, packed their families and their belongings into covered wagons and migrated west to settle the American frontier. Newspapers of the day profiled those intrepid souls risking everything for a plot of good farmland, with headlines trumpeting their pursuit of "The American Dream."

Significantly, federal policies explicitly encouraged and subsidized the great westward migration. The Homestead Act of 1862 promised early pioneers the right and title to 160 acres of undeveloped federal land west of the Mississippi River at no cost, provided that they agreed to improve the land and live on it for five years.

---

[31] John F. Kennedy, Message to Congress, February 27, 1962.

Even at the turn of the 20th century, farms, farm households and rural communities remained the norms in America, before they eventually succumbed to the effects of competition, industrialization, rising costs, and growing urbanization.

Figure 4 - U.S. Rural and Farm Population, 1900-2010

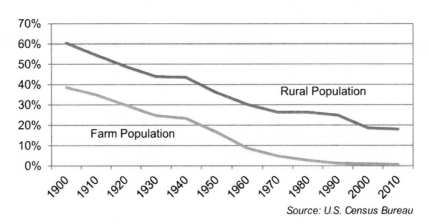

Source: U.S. Census Bureau

The point is that the specific components of the American Dream should be expected to change with the times. But the underlying drive to achieve a better life will always aim itself toward some specific economic and social goals, and the fulfillment of these goals will most likely be influenced, encouraged and supported by government policies.

Economic Components of the Modern American Dream

Today, the societal focus of the American Dream has shifted considerably. Not only has the single-family home replaced the farm as the ultimate goal and measure of middle-class prosperity, but we have added new requirements to the formula. I expect that most readers will agree that when we talk about the American Dream today, from an economic perspective, what we are chiefly talking about is the opportunity to:

- Own a home

- Get an education

- Have a good job or own a business

- Acquire a degree of wealth and financial security

This modern recipe for the American Dream is quite similar to one that Franklin D. Roosevelt outlined in his 1944 State of the Union address to Congress. To ensure the "pursuit of happiness" promised by the Declaration of Independence, FDR proposed a "Second Bill of Rights" guaranteeing each American:

> *The right to a useful and remunerative job in the industries or shops or farms or mines of the nation;*
>
> *The right to earn enough to provide adequate food and clothing and recreation;*
>
> *The right of every farmer to raise and sell his products at a return which will give him and his family a decent living;*
>
> *The right of every businessman, large and small, to trade in an atmosphere of freedom from unfair competition and domination by monopolies at home or abroad;*
>
> *The right of every family to a decent home;*
>
> *The right to adequate medical care and the opportunity to achieve and enjoy good health;*
>
> *The right to adequate protection from the economic fears of old age, sickness, accident, and unemployment;*
>
> *The right to a good education.*[32]

---

[32] Franklin D. Roosevelt, State of the Union Address, January 11, 1944.

Homeownership

Homeownership has become central to the American Dream for a variety of reasons. First, home ownership satisfies the basic human needs for shelter and protecting one's family.

Second, owning a home has long been heralded by financial experts as a smart investment whose value could be reliably counted on to increase year after year. As the humorist Will Rogers once said, "Buy land. They ain't making any more of the stuff!" Many families regard the money they put into their homes as a kind of forced savings – their nest egg – and the equity in their homes is the largest part of their net worth.

Homeownership also plays an important role in supporting families and building stable communities in America. Owning a home provides a family with "roots" for socialization and education, and a vested interest in the general welfare of the surrounding community and its local economy.

Finally, homeownership satisfies status needs for many individuals. It is a symbolic way of saying, "I made it," because at one time, owning a home was what separated the wealthy from the lower and middle socioeconomic classes. Today, of course, what separates the wealthy from others is more likely to be the location and size of their homes.

Homeownership is much more accessible in the U.S. than in many other countries, which is why it remains a defining characteristic of the American Dream. In some former communist countries, a family might have to wait years just to get a state apartment; and in many developed countries, homeownership remains a far-off dream because of high cost and the lack of credit. Also, by way of comparison, the size of the average American home is approximately

2400 square feet, while in India the average home is just 500 square feet and would house five people.[33]

Figure 5 - U.S. Homeownership Rate, 1900-2010

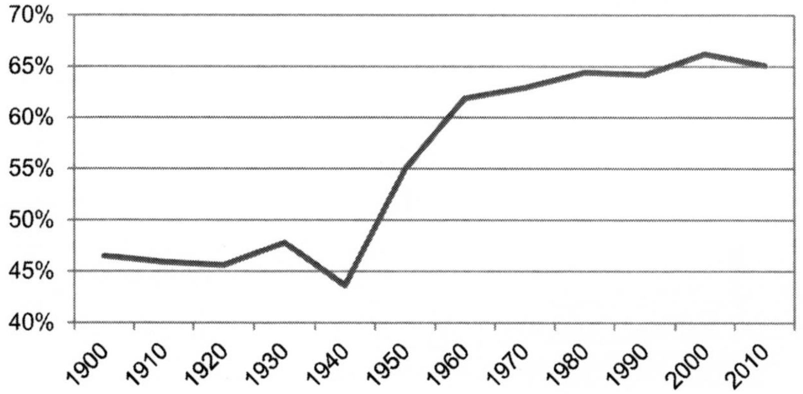

Source: U.S. Census Bureau

Education

As the son of parents who were both immigrants and educators, I grew up with a profound appreciation of the value that Americans place on education. Like many immigrants, my parents believed that everything they had – at least their material possessions – could be taken away from them at any moment. But what could never be taken away were things that, in our home, had enduring value and enabled one to build a better life: family, religion and education.

My parents made it clear that these were our priorities in life and we were expected to work hard at them. We were expected to be active in our church and make whatever sacrifices were necessary to support our family. But most of all, in education, we were expected

---

[33] For U.S. home size, see: U.S. Census Bureau, 2010. For Indian home size, see: Indian Ministry of Statistics and Programme Implementation, "Household Consumer Expenditure in India," *National Sample Survey 63rd Round*, June 2007.

to come home at the end of each term with a report card delivering straight A's. Anything less provoked disappointment and demanded explanation. These commitments were something that I carry with me today, and I have tried to pass the same values along to my children, particularly regarding education.

From a purely practical perspective, education in the U.S. is highly correlated with employment opportunities, job stability, and income, which all affect an individual's chances of achieving the prosperity of the American Dream. The majority of high-paying jobs in the U.S. require applicants to possess a bachelor's degree – or in some cases a professional degree – as the price of admission. In addition to its inherent economic value, having a higher education can also provide a degree of security. Unemployment is generally lower among college graduates than those whose highest educational attainment is high school or less. The following chart, from the Bureau of Labor Statistics, sums up the overall economic value of education quite clearly:

Figure 6 - Unemployment and Weekly Earnings by Educational Attainment, 2010

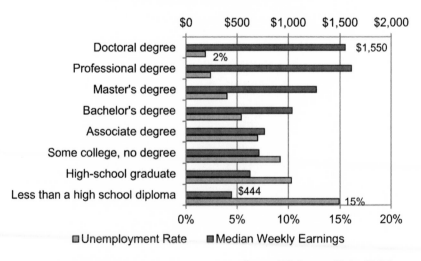

Source: U.S. Bureau of Labor Statistics

30

Education is important from a societal perspective, as well. It reinforces cultural identity, prepares individuals to become productive workers, enhances their status, and enables them to be responsible members of their communities. In many ways, it is the foundation of a strong and sustainable economy.

Employment and Entrepreneurism

The need to find or create gainful employment is as old and as basic as communities themselves. It is the primary means by which we exchange our labor and skills for capital, and contribute to building a diverse and sustainable economy. As I discussed in the previous chapter, the availability of employment and business opportunities played a crucial role in attracting immigrants to our country and enabling our communities to grow and flourish.

For some of us, gainful employment means finding a secure job that is interesting and financially rewarding with the potential for upward mobility. For others, it means starting a business where we can control our own destiny and our earning potential, participate directly in the marketplace, and build something of value.

Entrepreneurship has always been an essential part of the American character. We are eager to reward those who take risks and accept occasional failure as a natural consequence, without attaching a social stigma to it. This quality has made America a place where innovation and new ideas can thrive, nurturing economic growth, wealth accumulation and competition. It is no accident that more than 65% of net new jobs in America over the past 17 years – and most innovations – have come from small businesses.[34] Moreover, entrepreneurs accounted for 70% of the wealthiest Americans in 2011, according to the annual Forbes 400 list.[35]

---

[34] U.S. Small Business Administration, January 2011.
[35] *Forbes 400: The Richest People in America*, Forbes.com, September 21, 2011.

In addition to providing income, employment and business ownership provide a strong sense of purpose, giving structure and meaning to our daily lives and helping to define who we are. The opportunity to work and earn an income is a major part of fulfilling the American Dream.

Figure 7 - U.S. Unemployment Rate, 1950-2010

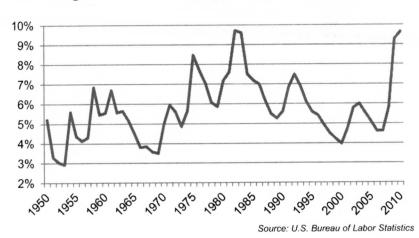

Source: U.S. Bureau of Labor Statistics

Wealth and Financial Security

In simpler times, Americans put great faith in the prospect of upward mobility, even if their expectation of wealth was not as great as it is today. A person was financially secure if they had enough money to put food on the table, provide shelter, and maintain the health of their family, and maybe leave a small inheritance.

Today, after earning (or borrowing) enough to buy a home, most Americans have an expectation of wealth, financial security and upward mobility that includes being able to send our kids to college, purchase a new car every few years, take extended vacations, receive annual salary increases and bonuses, invest in the stock market, acquire status goods and luxuries, enjoy a carefree retirement…and provide our children with a higher standard of living than our own.

Of course, wealth is what makes it possible to enjoy the fruits of a free society. For many of us, financial wealth is also the yardstick by which we gauge our success. At its best, the pursuit of wealth provides the motivation to engage in productive economic behavior and inspires the kinds of philanthropy exhibited by people like Warren Buffet and Bill Gates, who have donated substantial portions of their wealth to charitable causes. At its worst, the pursuit of wealth can give rise to excessive consumption and waste, tempting families to over leverage themselves into unsupportable levels of debt and engage in the American blood sport known as "Keeping up with the Joneses."

If you looked at the trend in median family income – a widely used measure of wealth – since World War II, it would be reasonable to conclude that Americans have been getting wealthier and wealthier all the time, thanks to a nearly unbroken upward trend line. But measuring our actual buying power is not so easy. Once we take into account the effect of inflation (as measured by changes in the CPI, or the Consumer Price Index), which eats away at the value of our dollars, it becomes clear that middle-class America has been basically treading water since 1975.

Figure 8 - Median Household Income/CPI, 1975-2010

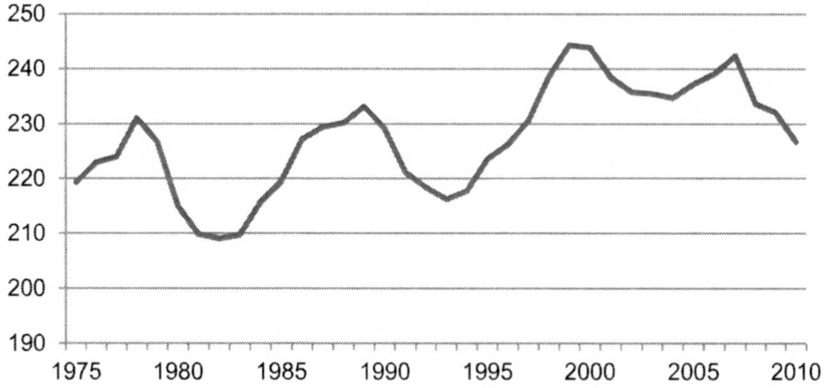

Source: U.S. Census Bureau & U.S. Bureau of Labor Statistics

33

Snapshot of the American Dream: Circa 2011

Here are some highlights to help summarize where we stand today in relation to the economic tenets of the American Dream:

- 65.1% of Americans own the homes they live in [36]

- 34.9% of Americans have a college or advanced degree [37]

- 59.9% of Americans aged 16 and older are employed [38]

- The average household income in America is $70,096.00 (2009 inflation-adjusted dollars) [39]

- Consumer spending makes up about 70% of U.S. economic activity [40]

- An estimated 552,600 new businesses were formed in the U.S. in 2009 [41]

- 41% of parents believe that their children will enjoy a higher standard of living than their own [42]

Do these numbers say anything about whether we are closer to fulfilling the American Dream? Not necessarily. We would need to look at these data points in the context of general economic trends over time and even across geographies before we could fully answer the question, "Are we better off today than we were yesterday?" And

---

[36] U.S. Census Bureau, 2010.
[37] Ibid.
[38] Ibid.
[39] Ibid.
[40] U.S. Dept. of Commerce.
[41] U.S. Small Business Administration.
[42] Ipsos survey sponsored by New York Life Insurance Company, May 2011.

even then, we would need to take into account whether people believe they enjoy greater upward mobility than in prior generations.

But consider, for comparison's sake, that in 1900 fewer than half of the people in America owned a home; 10.7% of the population was illiterate and the median level of educational attainment was the 8th grade; the average worker earned $12.98 a week for 59 hours of work; the average life expectancy was 47.3 years for women and 46.3 years for men; and there was no concept or expectation of comfortably retiring into one's golden years.

Credit and the American Dream

Regardless of how much better off we are today than yesterday, it would be hard to imagine any of the progress Americans have made in raising our overall standard of living without the support of government incentives and bank credit. This is particularly true for the small businesses, and consumers in the lower and middle socioeconomic classes.

In the next section, we will review the effect of government policies, incentives and spending programs in shaping the American Dream. But before we do, it's important to highlight the vital role that credit availability has played – and continues to play – in supporting the economic tenets of the American Dream.

The basic principle of credit – acquiring something of value today with the promise to pay for it at a future date – has always been fundamental to economic productivity and social well-being. It allows those with capital to lend it to others (while earning a premium for their risk), and allows those in need of capital to deploy it in profitable ways.

Credit has allowed explorers to finance journeys so that they could return with valuable commodities like gold, spices, and claims on new lands. It has allowed farmers to buy the seeds needed to plant the coming year's crops. It has given entrepreneurs the ability to finance the equipment, skilled personnel (whether software developers, researchers, or machine operators) and other resources needed to start and grow their businesses, along with the capital to expand and create additional jobs as their businesses grow.

For consumers, credit made it possible to afford the expensive goods produced during the industrial revolution, the appliances that afforded more time for leisure, the homes that gave families a place to live and made them part of a community, and the automobiles that made distant workplaces and vacation destinations accessible. Credit has also made it possible for many Americans to have college educations that were once available only to the wealthy.

Governments, wealthy individuals, manufacturers and merchants were once major providers of credit to businesses and consumers. But today, most credit is provided by the banks and other financial institutions that stand at the center of our local, national and global economies. Banks are the exchanges where those with capital can connect with those who have ideas for putting it to productive use.

Banks and the availability of credit have made it possible for people pursuing the American Dream to follow and accelerate their ambitions – by starting their businesses, buying their homes, or continuing their education. In facilitating each of these specific pursuits, credit also indirectly contributes to the growth of numerous other industries, including manufacturing, construction, publishing, insurance, financial services, and many more.[43] As such, each dollar of credit

---

[43] This "cascading" effect of credit also explains why, when credit becomes especially tight or freezes entirely, as it did during the financial crisis, the effect on business can be widespread and devastating.

can have an exponential effect on economic output. At the same time, the need for repayment by the borrower provides a powerful, ongoing motivation for productive individual effort and successful business management over the long term.

American Policy: Shaping the American Dream

Economic and public policies enacted over the past 80-plus years have been at least as influential as credit in shaping the modern version of the American Dream. Each presidential administration and each generation of policymakers has spearheaded initiatives aimed at bringing America closer to realizing our dream, whether through the introduction of bold social programs, or simply by undoing policies that weren't working. While history will show that not all policies have been wise or successful, most were born of good intentions.

To implement policy goals, Federal and State governments have relied mostly on two basic tools. One is incentives – in the form of tax credits, spending and entitlement programs – that make it economically attractive for the population to pursue one course of action over another. Because human beings are rational creatures, we respond fairly predictably to incentives. Just as the Homestead Act incentivized and influenced the pioneers to "Go west," policymakers in the 20th century have been able to use incentives such as R&D tax credits, the mortgage interest deduction and favorable treatment of capital gains to help us start businesses, purchase homes, invest in securities, and so on.

However, it seems to me that one of the great ironies of government incentives is that they are often cut or eliminated during the times when they would do the most good. Incentives generally encourage job creation through investment in new ideas, facilities and business expansion. This stimulates economic development while enabling businesses and individuals to pursue socially advantageous goals.

It can be argued that many incentives – especially those focused on business development – become more important, not less, when the economy is struggling through a difficult period, as it is today. But business incentives, subsidies and credits become easy targets for budget-cutting legislators who are willing to forego long-term benefits in return for short-term tax revenues.

The second key tool at the policymakers' disposal is regulation – essentially, a formal set of disincentives designed to control or prevent undesirable behavior, backed by the threat of significant penalties. Regulations generally flourish in areas of behavior and industries that are engaged in socially essential functions, such as transportation, employment, energy, agriculture, the environment, finance and banking.

In the pages that follow, I will outline some of the major policies and regulations that arose from the circumstances of our recent history and gave rise to the modern version of the American Dream. As we shall see, some eras actively promoted the dream's fulfillment, while others sought mainly to preserve and protect what had already been achieved. My goal is not to provide a complete history of U.S. economic policy during the 20th century, but rather to identify the major themes that have influenced our aspirations as a society. I will also discuss how certain policies, in striving to make the dream easier to attain, ironically have placed it out of reach for many Americans – and could potentially put it out of existence.

Depression, The New Deal, and the Eve of World War II

When Franklin D. Roosevelt took office in 1933, America was in the throes of a long and harrowing economic depression. The economy had stalled, more than 25% of American workers were unemployed, and nearly one-third of existing banks had failed. Surveying the state of the union, FDR saw a people who were dispirited, out of money, and out of work. He decided it was time to recalibrate both the American psyche and the American economy. He laid out a "New Deal" for America.

Fueled by vast, government-financed social programs, FDR sought to put an end to the Depression and reinvigorate the American Dream. He offered the promise of full employment, a robust economy, economic security for the elderly and unemployed, and a society where everyone could enjoy "the fruits of scientific progress in a wider and constantly rising standard of living."[44]

Roosevelt's efforts to fulfill this promise resulted in a succession of policies that touched nearly every corner of the economy. He created the Public Works Administration, the Works Progress Administration, and numerous other programs to provide Federal jobs for millions of unemployed workers. He created the Reconstruction Finance Corporation to lend financial support to railroads and manufacturers that were struggling in the contracted economy. He created the Securities and Exchange Commission to protect against corporate influence and corruption in the investment community. He signed the Glass-Steagall Act and created the Federal Deposit Insurance Corporation to help stabilize and strengthen the banking system. And he established the Social Security system to help older people meet their financial needs.

Each of these actions would prove to have a profound influence on America's economic and political landscape for years to come. Yet among the less heralded, but no less significant, of FDR's policies were those directed at stimulating home construction and making homeownership a cornerstone of the American Dream.

FDR recognized that demand for credit, furniture, refrigerators, stoves, utilities and other adjuncts to owning a home would deliver

---

[44] Franklin D. Roosevelt, State of the Union Address, January 6, 1941.

a significant and much needed boost to the economy. Incentivizing home buying also would help banks unload the large inventory of foreclosed homes they had amassed as housing demand and the ability of homeowners to pay off existing loans crashed with the rest of the economy during the Depression.

The foundation of FDR's housing policy was the creation of the Federal Housing Authority (FHA) under the 1934 National Housing Act. With the FHA, the government was able to set standards for home construction and, for the first time, began insuring mortgages. By offering insurance, the FHA made it possible for banks and other lenders to issue low interest, amortized loans that could be repaid over 25 to 30 years, as opposed to the 3- to 10-year balloon-type loans that were common at the time. With these terms – plus low down payment requirements – home ownership became suddenly affordable for more people than ever.

To further spur homeownership, FDR instituted a variety of large-scale, infrastructure programs – such as road and sewer construction projects – aimed at making living outside a city as practical and convenient as living within one.

On the financial front, FDR introduced numerous policies to reform and stabilize the banking system, protecting an institution that, as we have already seen, is the primary lubricant for the American Dream. In his first official act as President, FDR closed all national banks for an enforced three-day "holiday" to help defuse a growing bank panic. At the end of this holiday, he hurriedly introduced the Emergency Banking Act, which provided unlimited Treasury backing for all bank deposits.

Later that same year, FDR crafted a more substantial policy to address the banking system's problems. The Banking Reform Act of 1933, more commonly known as the Glass-Steagall Act, sought to clearly separate the activities of commercial banking and investment banking, requiring all banks to engage in one or the other and to limit their services accordingly.

The dividing line was mostly intended to prevent commercial banks from making the kinds of risky investments with their depositors' money that many people felt either caused or exacerbated the financial system's collapse during the Depression. The Act also sought to eliminate the conflict of interest that can exist when a single institution is simultaneously engaged in lending and investment activities. An example of this would be when a bank finances a company (perhaps with a less-than-pristine balance sheet) while at the same time encouraging depositors to buy shares in that company.

The Glass-Steagall Act also created the Federal Deposit Insurance Corporation (FDIC), which institutionalized the insurance of bank deposits. The FDIC initially insured deposits for up to $2,500 (increasing the amount to $5,000 six months later) and proved highly effective at quelling depositor fears of bank failure.

The Social Security Act was yet another New Deal program that had a lasting impact on the American Dream. Implemented in 1935, this program – funded exclusively by payroll taxes – provided Americans with a system of universal retirement payments, unemployment insurance, and welfare benefits for the poor and disabled. The program offered a degree of financial security to people whose ability to earn an income was diminished, and allowed all workers to entertain the idea of enjoying a sustained period of retirement near the end of their lives.

Post-World War II and the Boom Years

If we think of the New Deal as planting the seeds for achieving the American Dream, then the period from the end of World War II through the late-1960s was a time when many of those seeds bore fruit.

41

Just before America entered the war, FDR had refocused the country's industrial output toward our anticipated military needs. Manufacturing plants that produced automobiles were retooled to produce military vehicles. Clothing manufacturers switched over to making uniforms instead of business suits. The order books for shipbuilders and aircraft manufacturers swelled with new contracts for destroyers and bombers.

Economic output increased dramatically thanks to the huge number of new arms and manufacturing jobs, and unemployment reached a low of 2%. With much of the pre-war workforce engaged in fighting the war – approximately 12 million men were serving in the military – this period also saw unprecedented numbers of women and minorities entering the labor force to fill the gap that was left behind.

When the war ended, America emerged a much stronger nation – both spiritually and economically. We were pumped up from victories in Europe and the Pacific. Our economy had become the largest in the world. And we had built up an immense industrial infrastructure during the war that could now be returned to civilian purposes.

Although economic growth immediately following the war was not as strong as it had been during the war years, GDP continued to grow and the country did not sink into the prolonged recession that some people expected once the war ended.

Needless to say, a large number of young GI's had returned from the conflicts overseas with pent-up economic demand and the freedom once again to pursue their dreams in the civilian world. Like everyone else, they wanted a better education, jobs, homes, families, and maybe even businesses of their own. America owed an immense debt to these men, and it was a debt that we sought to repay through the G.I. Bill.

The G.I. Bill, created just before the end of the war, was like the American Dream in a box for returning servicemen. It provided free college tuition, allowing the vets to begin or finish their education and improve their career prospects. It provided one year of unemployment benefits to help them get back on their feet and reestablish their civilian lives, and generous, no-cost healthcare benefits. It also offered government-backed, no-money-down loans to help them buy homes, and low-cost loan programs to help them start businesses, if that's what they wanted to do.

As a result of the G.I. Bill, college enrollment took off. For the first time in the nation's history, access to a college education became something that wasn't the sole province of the wealthy; it was now readily available to the middle class. Home construction gained steam as huge tracts of affordable housing – like the iconic Levittown development on Long Island, NY – sprang up and established the template for today's sprawling suburban communities.

Automotive sales skyrocketed as Detroit returned its factories to the production of passenger cars. Durable goods manufacturers struggled to keep up with demand for refrigerators, stoves, washing machines and other appliances that were needed by a generation of new homeowners who were hungry to enjoy the material expressions of the American Dream.

The entire Post-war environment, from the mid-1940s until the 1970s, was in many ways a golden age in America's pursuit of happiness. It was a period when manufacturing was healthy, business conglomerates were being created through consolidation, and there was little foreign competition.

Exports of U.S. goods were strong, in part because the Marshall Plan had created a market for U.S. goods in Europe – to aid continental rebuilding efforts after the war – and also because the establishment of the International Monetary Fund (IMF) in 1944 made global trade between nations much easier.

Americans in the post-war years could reasonably expect to find long-term employment – either with local employers or the large corporations that dominated major industries from airlines and cars to telephone service – and achieve incremental improvements in their lifestyles, year after year. Many could even look forward to a pension to supplement their Social Security income when they retired.

Despite a few bumps along the way, the American standard of living was steadily increasing. The economy was growing (from about $200 million GDP in 1940 to more than $500 million in 1960), more people were getting a better education (with 33% of the population having a high-school diploma or more in 1947 versus more than 50% in the late 1960s), incomes were rising (from an average of just under $20,000 in 1947 to nearly $27,000 in 1960), and the stock market was chugging along nicely (with the Dow Jones Industrial Average increasing more than eight-fold, from 112.77 on January 2, 1942 to 969.26 on December 31, 1965). We also experienced the nation's largest increase in birthrates, resulting in today's massive generation of Baby Boomers.

Homeownership reached all-time highs during the post-war years, as well. According to the U.S. Census Bureau, approximately 62% of Americans owned a home in 1960 – almost a 40% increase over the homeownership rate in the 1930s. Among other things, the popularity of the automobile, sub-$20 barrel oil, and investments in the interstate highway system (under the Federal-Aid Highway Act of 1956), made it increasingly attractive for people to move out of the cities and buy new homes in the suburbs. Moreover, the availability of installment credit helped people quickly fill their homes with material goods appropriate to their upwardly mobile lifestyle and pay their purchases off over time.

From a purely social perspective, perhaps the culmination of the golden age of the American Dream came during the administration of Lyndon Johnson, following the assassination of John F. Kennedy in 1963. Johnson's vision of a "Great Society" produced an abundance of domestic policies focused on eliminating poverty and racial injustice – giving more people the opportunity to realize the American Dream – but also touching on education, medical care, urban renewal and transportation.

With the Economic Opportunity Act of 1964, Johnson launched a wide range of antipoverty programs, with a special emphasis on urban youth and the poor. These programs included the Job Corps, the Neighborhood Youth Corps, Project Head Start and Upward Bound; Volunteers in Service to America (VISTA); the Model Cities Program; the Food Stamp program; and the Community Action Program.

In addition, Johnson boosted federal assistance to elementary, secondary and higher education institutions; increased benefits and expanded coverage under the Social Security system; and introduced the Medicare and Medicaid programs, providing federal assistance for healthcare costs for the elderly and those receiving welfare payments.

The post-war years unfolded like a storybook tale of economic growth, prosperity and social progress, and it seemed like the good times might never end. But toward the end of the 1960s, storm clouds had begun to gather that were threatening to dampen the American Dream.

Inflation, Globalization and Deregulation

Despite years of increasing prosperity and huge government expenditures on social programs, Richard Nixon took office in 1969 amidst lingering unrest among the urban poor, unresolved civil rights issues, and growing anger over the seemingly interminable

Vietnam War. On the economic side, our nation was struggling with high inflation and numerous problems related to globalization that threatened to diminish the American people's pursuit of happiness.

Figure 9 - Unemployment and Inflation Rates, 1960-2010

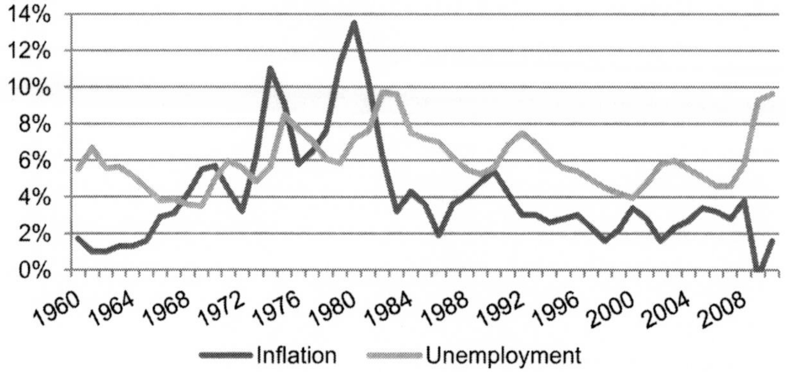

Source: U.S. Bureau of Labor Statistics

Inflation was a particularly troublesome problem. It was seriously eroding the purchasing power of the dollar, slowing the economy, and contributing to high levels of unemployment. Simultaneously, the cost of sustaining the numerous social programs that were enacted during more prosperous times had begun to weigh heavily on the Federal budget. Like new taxes, such programs proved easy to launch but nearly impossible to scale back.

In an attempt to control inflation before he entered his campaign for re-election, Nixon took the bold step of imposing wage and price controls and taking the U.S. off the gold standard in 1971. These radical moves did help to reduce inflation for a time, but the problem returned again two years later, exacerbated by the nation's first major oil crisis and a stock market crash. Another round of price controls followed, but these, too, failed to eliminate the problem.

Inflation remained a drag on the economy throughout the Ford and Carter administrations, as well. Unemployment, which had declined through most of the 1960s, trended upward repeatedly during the early and late 1970s, in lockstep with inflation.

At the same time that Americans' wealth was being eaten away by inflation, the country was being awakened to the new realities of a global economy. While post-war America once stood head and shoulders above other countries in manufacturing and economic might, our neighbors in Europe and Asia were quickly catching up. By 1971, America's enormous appetite for many goods and resources – especially oil – had outstripped our domestic manufacturing supplies and drilling capabilities, and we became a net importer.

Foreign companies were eager to tap into the hungry U.S. market, and American manufacturers were forced to contend with increasing competition from imported goods, including automobiles and electronics. In many instances, these foreign companies' prices were hard to match, in part because domestic firms were burdened with greater regulation and bloated cost structures.

Figure 10 - U.S. Trade Balance, 1960-2010
($ Billions)

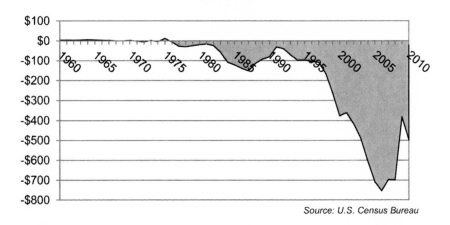

Source: U.S. Census Bureau

The demand for oil was a particular concern in America's emerging reliance on global trade because it increased our exposure to political and economic events in other parts of the world. During the 1973 Arab oil embargo, crude prices increased to over $40 per barrel, resulting in gasoline shortages in the U.S. and long lines at gas stations across the country. Continuing disruptions in the Middle East during the late 1970s and early '80s, which culminated in the Iran/Iraq war, caused oil prices to shoot upward again, this time reaching over $70 per barrel, with negative repercussions throughout the economy.

Figure 11 - U.S. Crude Oil Imports, 1920-2010
(Thousand Barrels per Day)

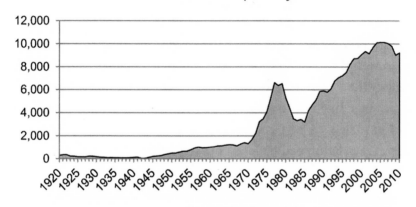

Source: U.S. Energy Information Administration

One striking example of how all these forces – inflation, recession, unemployment, foreign competition and rising oil prices – converged in the late 1970s was the near-bankruptcy and (first) bailout of the Chrysler Corporation, one of America's Big Three automakers and the 10th largest company in the U.S. at the time.

In 1979, gasoline prices were hovering around $1.10 a gallon, roughly double the price it had sold for during the previous 60 years. Chrysler was an old-line manufacturer known for building big, gas guzzling land yachts. Because of the high gas prices, demand for Chrysler's cars withered. Families, who were already struggling with high mortgage rates and rising costs for just about everything else, had decided that cheaper and thriftier Japanese imports were a much better alternative. Chrysler's revenue declined severely and its lack of available cash – combined with the wage demands of a unionized workforce – made it likely that the company would soon be unable to maintain its daily operations.

Chrysler executives and union leaders appealed to the Federal government for assistance, arguing that a Chrysler failure would have far-reaching and unacceptable repercussions across the entire U.S. economy. Its "Too Big to Fail" argument was one that reverberates even more painfully to Americans today.

The government, in a controversial decision, agreed to provide Chrysler with $1.2 billion in loans to save the company while demanding significant wage concessions from Chrysler workers. While the bailout did allow Chrysler to get back on its feet, the controversy didn't go away. A column in *Time* magazine wondered aloud about the message that Chrysler's bailout had sent to American business:

> *The congressional debate will resurrect all the arguments for and against giving federal aid to any company. There is a strong case that such help rewards failure and penalizes success, puts a dull edge on competition, is unfair to an ailing company's competitors and their shareholders, and inexorably leads the Government deeper into private business. Why should a huge company be bailed out, say critics, while thousands of smaller firms suffer bankruptcy every year? Where should the Government draw the line? GM Chairman Thomas A. Murphy has attacked federal help for Chrysler as "a basic challenge to the philosophy of America.* [45]

To shore up America's competitiveness in the global economy and avoid the need for future bailouts like Chrysler's, government policies

---

[45] "Business: Chrysler's Crisis Bailout," *Time*, August 20, 1979.

began to focus in earnest on deregulating certain industries during the 1970s and '80s, while reducing the regulatory burdens on others. The government appeared to have taken the view that, despite any risks, American business was healthier when guided by market forces, rather than government controls. Some of the most important deregulation efforts of this period included:

- 1977 – **Natural Gas**: The Emergency Natural Gas Act of 1977

- 1978 – **Airlines**: The Airline Deregulation Act

- 1978 – **Natural Gas**: National Gas Policy Act of 1978

- 1980 – **Savings and Loans**: The Depository Institutions Deregulation and Monetary Control Act of 1980

- 1980 – **Small Business**: The Regulatory Flexibility Act

- 1980 – **Railroads and Trucking**: The Staggers Rail Act and the Motor Carrier Act of 1980

- 1982 – **Savings and Loans**: Garn–St. Germain Depository Institutions Act of 1982

- 1982 – **Interstate Buses**: Bus Regulatory Reform Act of 1982

- 1984 – **Ocean Shipping:** The Ocean Shipping Act of 1984 (and later, the Ocean Shipping Reform Act of 1998)

- 1986 – **Freight Forwarders:** Surface Freight Forwarder Deregulation Act of 1986

It wasn't until the Reagan administration in the 1980s that America finally got inflation under control. Reagan's supply-side (or "trickle-down") economic policies employed a combination of tax cuts, reduced federal spending and tighter control of the money supply, with the goal of encouraging business investment and reducing interest rates. Reagan believed that a more favorable business climate would allow the country to resume its growth, while creating higher employment and higher wages.

During his two terms in office, Reagan implemented many policies that were instrumental in deregulating business and encouraging investment, and he authorized numerous programs to prepare disadvantaged youth to become part of the American labor force.

Overall, Reagan's supply-side economic policies were immensely successful in getting the economy back on track and reducing unemployment. But the cost of conquering inflation, boosting GDP, attacking the pressures of increased global competition and financing massive Cold War defense expenditures ultimately led to higher federal and trade deficits.

Likewise, the deregulation initiatives introduced by Reagan and his predecessors freed up American business to be more competitive. But deregulation created problems of its own, such as the Savings and Loan crisis in the 1980s, when 747 out of the 3,234 savings and loan associations in the United States failed...at a cost of nearly $124 billion to U.S. taxpayers.[46]

After Congress limited the savings rate that banks could pay on deposits in 1966, the S&Ls – which had financed most of the post-World War II housing boom – found themselves at a disadvantage in attracting deposits when higher interest rates were being offered by other types of financial institutions. Recognizing that the financial health of the S&Ls was at risk, Congress passed deregulation measures in 1980 and 1982, expanding the thrifts' lending authority

---

[46] Timothy Curry and Lynn Shibut, "The Cost of the Savings and Loan Crisis: Truth and Consequences," *FDIC Banking Review*, Vol. 13 No. 2 (Washington, DC: Federal Deposit Insurance Company, 2000).

and the array of savings products they could offer, and subjecting them to "looser" accounting rules.

The result, as some readers may remember, was that many S&Ls became involved in ever-riskier ventures and loan programs to support their higher savings rates. When a number of these loans and ventures went south, huge capital problems ensued, leading to widespread failures and, eventually, the need for a massive bailout through the Resolution Trust Corporation.

Many people blamed the S&L crisis and the resulting slowdown in the financial and real estate markets for a steep drop in new home sales – from 1.8 million to 1 million – that occurred between 1986 and 1991.

Two other major policy decisions from this period need to be mentioned because of their effect on banks and credit unions, and their effect on the tenets of the American Dream. The first was the Community Reinvestment Act of 1977, which sought to eliminate the practice of "redlining" (refusing to issue loans to borrowers in low- to moderate-income neighborhoods) by ensuring that commercial banks and savings associations serve the needs of borrowers across all segments of their communities, within the bounds of prudent risk. While the Act was no doubt intended to prevent discrimination, it became a driving force behind the large number of sub-prime mortgages that were issued over the next 30 years, many of which eventually imploded.

The second key piece of legislation during this time was the Gramm-Leach-Bliley Act (GLBA) of 1999, which effectively repealed the provisions of the 1933 Glass-Steagall Act and eliminated all remaining barriers between commercial and investment banking. The legislation was intended primarily to make U.S. banks more competitive with overseas banks that were less heavily regulated, and to provide U.S. banks with additional sources of non-interest income.

From this point onward, banks and bank holding companies were free to engage in retail banking, investment banking, insurance and numerous other forms of finance and lending. It was GLBA, more than anything else, that permitted already-large banks like Citicorp, Bank of America, Wells Fargo and others to take on additional lines of business and merge with other companies to become "Too Big to Fail."

The Indebted American Consumer

Throughout much of the 1970s, '80s and '90s, American consumers seemed unfazed or blissfully ignorant of the economic problems that were swirling all around them. Consumers seemed to assume that it was every American's right to possess the full measure of the American Dream, rather than every American's opportunity to fulfill their individual potential through hard work and sacrifice.

Because we increasingly felt entitled to the economic tenets of the American Dream, Americans continued to live and spend as if the economy were still in the 1950s boom times. Many of us were living beyond our means, rather than within them. And one of the chief reasons we could keep this party going was because we had access to easier forms of credit.

Starting in the late 1960s, revolving credit became widely available to the American consumer, in the form of the wallet-sized credit cards. Americans liked the convenience of the cards, which freed them from the need to carry large amounts of cash and the hassle of writing checks, and credit cards quickly became a popular way to purchase everyday items. In 1970, 16% of U.S. families had a bank credit card; by 1990 nearly 60% of U.S. families did.[47] Total revolving debt in the U.S. in 1968 was $1.3 billion; by 1990 it ballooned to $238.6 billion.[48]

---

[47] U.S. Federal Reserve, Annual Survey of Consumer Finance, 1970.
[48] U.S. Federal Reserve, G.19 Consumer Credit Data Set, Federal Reserve Statistical Release.

Banks, too, liked the cards, because they generated transaction fees and carried much higher interest rates than other types of loans for consumers who carried a balance.

Figure 12 - U.S. Per Capita Non-Real Estate Consumer Debt, 1950-2010

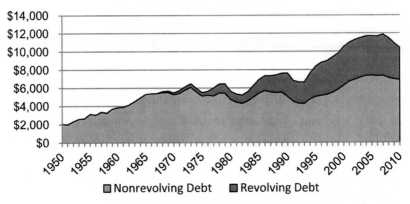

Source: U.S. Federal Reserve & U.S. Bureau of Labor Statistics

Credit cards were just one way to finance our lifestyle. As more and more people became homeowners, they soon discovered that they could "tap" their home equity through home equity loans and lines of credit, as well as cash-out refinancing. These types of arrangements, which started gaining popularity during the 1980s, seemed like a painless way to profit from rising home values without having to sell the underlying assets.

But consumer borrowing was riskier than we knew because it was based on two incorrect assumptions. The first was a belief in perpetual upward mobility. This belief, in fact, underlies most lending, which assumes that a borrower will be able to sustain or increase his or her earnings over time, and be in a position to pay back the loan. However, bouts of unemployment, wage concessions, mounting debt burdens and other factors continually prove that this is not always the case.

Responsible Lending – Putting on the Brakes...

As a local credit union, we want to help people make responsible financial decisions. Sometimes that means putting people before profits, which is exactly what we did during a promotional event we sponsored with several local auto dealers to finance new car loans.

A young man was caught up in the event's carnival atmosphere. I could tell he was overwhelmed with excitement and feeling pressure from a salesman to purchase a new truck. It was a fancy and expensive truck with giant wheels. The glimmer in this 18-year-old's eye was clearly blinding him from the huge loan payment.

Because I have children, my nurturing instinct kicked in; I was worried he was taking on more than he could handle. When the dealer walked away, I approached the young man and introduced myself. He told me he had a job, but no budget. I asked if he had considered ancillary expenses like sales tax, registration and fees; he had not. I told him what insurance would cost, and he was stunned.

Assuming the parental role, I said "This is a very big decision for you and you should think about it overnight." I had a moral responsibility to make sure he didn't feel pressured to buy something beyond his means. I wasn't trying to talk him out of the truck. I just wanted to make sure he was making the deal with his eyes wide open, knowing that a bad experience now could set off a spiral of financial despair that could last years.

The young man left and the dealer was furious. Whether they met again to make the deal, I'm not sure. But I am certain I acted in the best interest of this young man, because I was just as concerned for him as I would be for my own family.

Carrie Birkhofer, President and CEO
Bay Federal Credit Union

★ ★ ★

The second flawed assumption was that asset values – particularly home values and stock prices – would trend inexorably higher. This helps to explain why U.S. consumers were so willing to go into debt with homes and their credit cards. They "knew" that these assets would increase in value over time, and that even with the effects of inflation, they would be able to repay their debt in cheaper future dollars.

This assumption, too, proved false when the dot.com market bubble crashed in the year 2000, causing stocks to lose some 50% to 75% of the growth they had achieved in the 1990s, and again when the housing bubble burst in 2006. What most Americans failed to realize was they had lost touch with the realities of the economy and the American Dream, and been overtaken by the kind of "irrational exuberance" that former Fed Chairman Alan Greenspan warned against in a 1996 speech.[49]

Figure 13 - NASDAQ Closing Price, 1971 – 2011

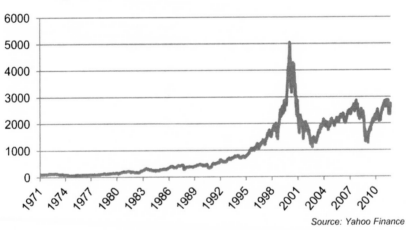

Source: Yahoo Finance

Long before Greenspan made his comments, however, President Carter had also chided Americans for losing touch with our funda-

---

[49] Alan Greenspan, Speech to the American Enterprise Institute, Washington, DC, December 5, 1996.

mental American values. In a televised address in 1979, known as the "crisis in confidence speech" (or the "malaise speech"), he said:

> *In a nation that was proud of hard work, strong families, close-knit communities and our faith in God, too many of us now tend to worship self-indulgence and consumption. Human identity is no longer defined by what one does, but by what one owns. But we've discovered that owning things and consuming things does not satisfy our longing for meaning.*[50]

This was not the message America wanted to hear, and some say it cost Carter the 1980 election.

Prescription for a Stronger Community...

The American Dream has fueled the entrepreneurial spirit for decades. It's the idea or spark that ignites a passion in someone to start a business. I saw that spark in a couple that left a chain pharmaceutical company and life in the city to open a corner drug store in northern Minnesota. They carried heavy debt, were building a home and didn't have much to invest in the business. And they came to me for a small business loan.

The husband and wife were both licensed pharmacists. They were well prepared with demographic data, a business plan that targeted a particular niche and a credible, ten-year earnings projection. I approved a two million dollar loan, stepping out on a limb when other banks wouldn't work with them. As a community banker, I had the flexibility to factor in good character and a creative business plan when I made this loan decision.

(continued on next page)

---

[50] Jimmy Carter, Malaise Speech to the American Public, June 30, 1979.

This couple and their corner drug store were going up against the big chains, but they created a unique niche and served the market in creative and personal ways that the national pharmacies simply ignored. I'm glad we made the loan because the business hit a home run. The loan has been largely paid off, the drug store is profitable, and they've created many good paying jobs in our community. They have a sustainable business model and today they are the best player in the market. I'm happy to have seen them execute so well when the big banks wouldn't talk to them.

The American Dream gives entrepreneurs a chance, and so do I. As a community banker, I am able to help people realize their dreams. This gives me continued hope for a stronger community, and Main Street America needs a whole lot more of that.

Noah W. Wilcox, President and CEO
Grand Rapids State Bank

★ ★ ★

3: The Financial Crisis

"No good deed goes unpunished." [51]
Clare Booth Luce

Looking back, one might easily have predicted the financial crisis that began in 2007 – when the housing market collapsed, pushing banks, businesses and the world economy near the brink of disaster – as the natural consequence of policy decisions and economic trends that had been mounting for decades. Government policy to increase home ownership, the federal policy to allow inexpensive credit and the very drive for more wealth all converged to create the imbalance that caused the sub-prime crisis and the subsequent global economic crisis.

What's ironic is that most of these policies and trends were a direct outgrowth of well-intentioned efforts to help citizens achieve the American Dream. But they ultimately led to a situation in the U.S. that had a negative impact on nearly every aspect of the American Dream, from housing to jobs to wealth. So, what went wrong?

Call it "too much of a good thing."

For one thing, policies that had evolved over nearly 70 years made homeownership seem like a fundamental right of all Americans, rather than a privilege earned through hard work and saving. Throughout the housing boom, low interest rates (averaging less than 7% from 2002 onward), low down payments and lax underwriting standards

---

[51] Claire Booth Luce, in Harold Faber, *The Book of Laws* (New York: Times Books, 1979).

made getting a mortgage unbelievably easy and affordable for nearly anyone.

Figure 14 - Federal Funds Rate, 1954-2011

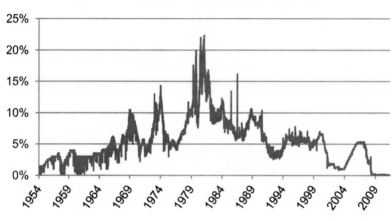

Source: U.S. Federal Reserve

The policies that promoted this lending environment coincided meaningfully with the American desire for upward mobility. Families who previously believed that they couldn't afford a home now learned that this milestone of the American dream was within their grasp. Of course, this had less to do with any improvement in their own prospects and more to do with the easy credit policies at Fannie Mae and Freddie Mac (which, together with the FHA, support more than 90% of all new mortgage loans) and the non-redlining directives of the Community Reinvestment Act of 1977, which encouraged lending in largely subprime neighborhoods.[52] A variety of ill-considered financing arrangements, such as interest-only and so-called NINJA (No Income, No Job or Assets) loans, also helped bring homeownership to a wider segment of the population than ever before. Lenders could be heard pitching their wares like late-night infomercial hosts: "No money? No job? No problem!"

---

[52] Binyamin Appelbaum, "Without Loan Giants, 30-Year Mortgage May Fade Away," *New York Times*, March 3, 2011.

Challenges Ahead for Fannie Mae and Freddie Mac

Fannie Mae and Freddie Mac are entities that make credit continually available for mortgage lending. They accomplish this by buying mortgages from banks and securitizing them into mortgage-backed securities (MBS) that are sold to private investors. By buying up existing mortgages, Fannie and Freddie make mortgage funds available to reinvest again in more lending.

Fannie Mae started as a government entity in the 1930s, to boost the housing market at a time when banks were unable to do so. But as it played a larger role in the mortgage financing market and its debt obligations swelled – from decades of pro-homeownership policies – the government felt compelled to take Fannie's obligations off the government's books. In 1968, the government split Fannie into two organizations: a publicly held enterprise retaining the name Fannie Mae that invested in the private mortgage market; and Ginnie Mae, a government enterprise that was established to guarantee FHA, VA and other types of mortgage loans. In 1970, the government also created Freddie Mac as a competitor to Fannie Mae, essentially to prevent a monopoly.

As Government Sponsored Enterprises (GSEs), Fannie and Freddie are quasi-governmental private companies that enjoy special privileges and advantages in the mortgage market. First, they have nearly unlimited access to U.S. Treasury funds at rates far lower than a bank or other lenders can get. Secondly, they are exempt from state and local income taxes, as well as from SEC oversight and reporting. They also enjoy the financial protection of the U.S government, which makes their creditworthiness unassailable and implies that they will never be allowed to fail.

(continued on next page)

During the housing crisis, it became clear that the assets underlying Fannie's and Freddie's mortgage-backed securities were in trouble and the companies' business was at risk from mounting defaults. To protect the mortgage market from implosion, the government reclaimed control of Fannie and Freddie in 2008, placing them into the conservatorship of the Federal Housing Finance Association – even though both were technically private companies.

Today, taxpayers are on the hook for more than $182 billion in bailouts to Fannie and Freddie through the Troubled Assets Relief Program (TARP). Unlike banks, which received $236 billion through TARP, and repaid $215 billion (91%) of their TARP funds – plus $30 billion more in taxpayer dividends, warrants and interest – Fannie and Freddie have not repaid any of their TARP funding.

We still don't know to what extent the American taxpayer will end up footing the bill for all the bad mortgages that Fannie and Freddie guaranteed, and whether or not both organizations will ultimately be allowed to fail. There are no simple answers.

It is clear that Fannie and Freddie expanded far beyond their original mandate. By the end of 2007, they and the Federal Home Loan Banks provided 90% of the financing for new mortgages. The private market had been essentially squeezed out.

At the same time, as quasi-public entities, these organizations' business decisions are inevitably tinged by political considerations. For example, by mid-year 2007 Freddie held more than $120 billion in sub-prime mortgages. This extraordinary level of risk was not dictated by private-sector business decisions, but by

(continued on next page)

government policy considerations and political calculations. The end result was not good, as we are all too painfully aware.

The essential question is whether any "quasi-public" organization can make decisions based on sound economic and business considerations, free of political calculation. Fannie and Freddie could not. The individuals who ran these organizations were appointed, at least in part, based on their political influence and standing rather than their knowledge of the mortgage markets. Moreover, they were not subject to the penalties that the market imposes on failure, other than the loss of their positions. Contrast this with Dick Fuld, former CEO of Lehman Brothers, whose failure cost him his company, his job, and a significant part of his net worth.

That said, Fannie and Freddie do play an important role in the U.S. housing market. The United States is one of the very few countries that does a large volume of home financing over long time horizons (often 30 years) at a fixed rate. This preferred financing shifts significant interest rate risk from the borrower to the lender, and few lenders are willing to accept this risk, correctly looking at the massive failure of the thrift industry in the 1980s that arose from it. Fannie and Freddie serve as the bridge between those consumers who prefer the stability of a long-term fixed rate mortgage, and investors (such as insurance companies) who seek long-term, stable investments like Mortgage Backed Securities.

Without Fannie and Freddie, U.S. home financing would probably become more like the rest of the world, with adjustable mortgage rates becoming the norm. This has implications not only for borrowers, but also for investors who prefer MBSs and other

(continued on next page)

long-term securities. Home financing rates would also be likely to rise, since Fannie and Freddie's government backing effectively reduces borrowing costs.

In the short term, the losses that Fannie and Freddie have and will continue to generate will be borne by the taxpayer. Since it is unlikely that we will see a rapid escalation in real estate values any time in the next three to five years, these losses are likely to be significant. What we need to do now is to make the hard decisions as to the long-term fate of Fannie and Freddie.

If we decide that America requires long-term fixed rate financing, the need for entities such as Fannie and Freddie is inevitable, given the role they play as the conduit between borrowers and investors that prefer MBS-type investments. However, we need to make certain that these entities are immune from the political machinations that led to the current situation. They should be restricted from accepting any type of subprime paper. Subprime and Alt-A lending serve an important role in our economic system by providing home financing to individuals with damaged or limited credit histories, as well as credit for entrepreneurs. It just is not a role that should be filled by the federal government.

Bill Handel, Vice President of Research
Raddon Financial Group

★ ★ ★

The lending environment also provided people who already owned homes with new ways to take advantage of the low interest rate environment. Using cash-out refinancing, home equity loans and other financial vehicles, they were able to tap the equity sitting in homes whose values, according to the U.S. Census Bureau, had risen year after year from 1970 through the early part of 2006 (or from 1997 to 2006, adjusted for inflation).

This perfect storm of favorable government policies, low mortgage rates and rapidly rising home values also made real estate the preferred game for investors and individuals seeking to make a quick buck. "Flipping" homes became such a popular pastime that it gave birth to a highly rated cable television series and inspired just about anyone with a few thousand dollars and a paintbrush to get in on the game.

It is easy to understand why banks participated in the flurry of mortgage lending that took place prior to the housing bust. First of all, they were encouraged to do so by government policies. Secondly, they were able to diversify their risk by selling their mortgages to the government-sponsored entities of Fannie Mae and Freddie Mac. And finally, as margins on their traditional businesses were shrinking, banks found a way to profit from cheap capital as the Federal Reserve systematically lowered federal funds rates from approximately 6% in 2000 to about 1% in 2004.

Overall, mortgage financing – along with auto, credit card and other types of financing – was a thriving business throughout the 1990s and early 2000s. Consumers opted to fast-track their way to financial security and a better lifestyle, even though it involved taking on new (albeit low-cost) debt. In fact, according to The Economist, U.S. household debt had risen to 127% of annual disposable personal income by the end of 2007.[53]

Another important factor that contributed to the financial crisis was the passage of the Gramm-Leach-Bliley Act (GLBA) in 1999. This Act, designed to diversify the risk and increase the competitiveness of America's financial institutions, tore down the "invisible wall" created by Glass-Steagall and allowed financial institutions to

---

[53] "The End of the Affair," *The Economist*, October 30, 2008.

combine commercial banking activities with investment banking and insurance operations. Unfortunately, the side effect of GLBA was that it introduced higher levels of risk into the economy and the financial system, and opened the floodgates to a series of financial industry mergers that created the massive entities ultimately deemed "Too Big to Fail."

Large banks probably felt little choice but to grow and take on additional risk. Market demands and competitive pressures were pushing them in the direction of becoming integrated financial services providers. At the same time, the sustained low interest rate environment had made banks desperate to find sources of non-interest fee income to maintain their historic levels of profitability.

The final catalyst for the financial crisis was Wall Street's concentrated focus on marketing derivatives based on pools of mortgage debt. The formula for these types of securities was not new – similar derivatives had existed for some time, with underlying debt assets based on everything from car loans to credit card receivables. What made mortgage loans – and particularly subprime mortgage loans – such fertile ground for investment was the volume of mortgage lending taking place at the time. This massive amount of debt represented rich streams of payments that could be packaged and resold as mortgage backed securities (MBSs) and collateralized debt obligations (CDOs), allowing U.S. and foreign investors – particularly cash-rich investors from the Middle East, China and Japan – to participate in and profit from the sub-prime housing boom.

To back the derivatives, the investment-bank sponsors borrowed money at low interest rates to buy up huge stockpiles of mortgages from large banks and mortgage lenders like Citibank, Bank of America, Countrywide, New Century, and so on. The sponsors then pooled these mortgages, sliced the pool into tranches representing different levels of risk with corresponding yields, sold the stream of payments to investors, and earned substantial fees for their efforts.

Wall Street wasn't the only group that loved MBSs and CDOs. The banks and mortgage lenders welcomed them, too. Banks were already under pressure from a changing business model that required sources other than traditional lending and fee income to generate profits. Selling off a portion of their subprime mortgage portfolio transferred default risk to third parties, gave the lenders fresh capital that they could funnel back into new loans and investments, and provided a stream of fee income from servicing the sold-off mortgages.

The pricing and safety of the MBSs and CDOs were based on models that assumed a continued rise in housing prices and the probability that only a small percentage of the subprime loans would default at any given time. Together, these two assumptions made each pool of loans seem reasonably safe. And to make some CDOs even safer, the investment bankers bought credit default insurance (swaps) to protect against unforeseen losses.

The credit rating agencies went along with the sponsors' logic – and earned their own high fees – as they granted the vast majority of subprime and Alt-A mortgage derivatives investment-grade, AAA ratings. The high ratings made toxic MBSs and CDOs appear relatively benign, and made them marketable to investors who otherwise would not have touched them. Neither Wall Street nor the credit rating agencies (Moody's, Standard & Poor's, and Fitch Ratings) who are their customers wanted to kill the goose that laid the golden egg. And neither envisioned the possibility of a total collapse in the housing market.

Figure 15 - New Home Sales Prices, 1965-2010

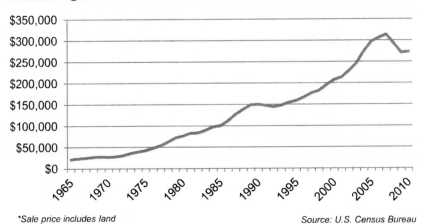

Sale price includes land   Source: U.S. Census Bureau

When the housing collapse that nobody imagined finally came to be in 2006, the whole, immense house of cards began falling down. More and more subprime loans went into default. Banks foreclosed on the properties and were left with homes instead of mortgages. The large number of foreclosures caused the value of other homes to fall, resulting in even more defaults and people walking away from homes that were now "underwater."

The sponsors, stuck with a growing inventory of depreciating homes and less money coming in from mortgages, found that they couldn't afford to make payments to investors on existing CDOs – and they couldn't find anyone willing to buy new CDOs to get rid of their unsold inventory of mortgages. Worse yet, the banks' creditors – who lent them the money to buy mortgages in the first place – demanded additional collateral to compensate for the reduced value of the banks' assets. It added up to a classic "squeeze" on the investment bankers, and its effects spread to their investors, insurers and creditors, as well.

The scenario was obviously more complicated than what I've briefly outlined here, and human greed played a significant role, but it's clear what happened next.

- Banks, financial institutions, pension funds, sovereign wealth funds and investors worldwide saw trillions of dollars disappear as their supposedly "safe" mortgage derivatives defaulted or lost most of their value. Many were forced to go bankrupt and were unable to meet their liquidity needs

- Credit markets froze up as doubt emerged surrounding banks' solvency and exposure to troubled mortgage securities

- The government's Troubled Asset Relief Program authorized expenditures of $700 billion to prop up banks and other parts of the financial system by purchasing their troubled assets

- Fannie Mae and Freddie Mac – the owners of significant amounts of subprime mortgage debt – were placed into government conservatorship and funded with $5.2 trillion in loan guarantees to cover their mortgage exposure

- Lehman Brothers, the fourth largest investment bank in the U.S., declared bankruptcy and was liquidated

- Bear Stearns and Merrill Lynch collapsed and were acquired for pennies on the dollar by JPMorgan Chase and Bank of America, respectively

- Wachovia, the fourth-largest bank holding company in the U.S., was taken over by Wells Fargo in a forced sale to prevent bankruptcy, while Bank of America rescued Countrywide Financial from a complete implosion

- Washington Mutual Bank, the largest savings and loan association in the U.S., was seized and placed it into receivership of the FDIC

- AIG, the 29th-largest public company in the world, was effectively taken over by the Federal Reserve Bank to pay off massive claims on its CDO credit default swaps

- The Dow Jones Industrial Average lost more than half of its value, dropping from 14,000 points in October 2007 to 6,600 by March 2009

- The U.S. entered into the worst recession in the past 50 years, as measured by changes in unemployment and the level of real GDP

The repercussions of the financial crisis weren't just limited to the U.S. financial markets. The crisis was magnified by the interconnectedness of capital markets worldwide and exacerbated by the fact that the housing market (and the other businesses it supports) had become such a disproportionate part of the U.S. economy. As a result, it shook the foundations of governments and markets around the globe. Equally important, the crisis dealt a major setback to the tenets of the American Dream. Over eight million jobs were lost, housing prices plummeted, small businesses failed, credit disappeared, personal savings vanished, and many people lost faith in America's leaders, regulators and financial institutions.

Warning Signs in the Rear-View Mirror

It is somewhat surprising that America was so remarkably unprepared for the financial crisis when it hit. Not long before, we had been through the dot.com boom and bust, and many people believed that the housing market was showing signs of being similarly overheated. There was active debate about the growing risks of subprime lending and mortgage derivatives, even from those within the industry. And more than a few people had become concerned about the size of America's largest financial institutions, as well as the amount of debt being carried by Fannie and Freddie. But when the times seemed so good and prosperous, it was easy to dismiss the warning signs and assure people that "this time was different."

Nevertheless, there were smart people who anticipated the coming crisis and raised their voices early on.

For instance, Dean Baker, an economist, managed to call the housing bubble in 2002. In a briefing paper, he noted that home values had fallen completely out of sync with nearly every economic measure against which they had been historically correlated. This kind of behavior, he said, amounted to a bubble – not dissimilar to the dot. com bubble that had recently burst. Baker warned that the long-term effects of this housing bubble would be a decline in construction and related industries, families caught flat-footed as their home equity suddenly disappeared, and other repercussions causing immense harm to the overall economy:

> *The economy will lose an important source of demand as housing construction plummets and the wealth effect goes into reverse. This will slow an economy already reeling from the effects of the collapse of the stock bubble. The loss of housing equity will be yet another blow to baby boomers on the edge of retirement, many of whom just endured large losses in the stock market.*[54]

Warren Buffet, Chairman of Berkshire Hathaway and one of the most successful investors of all time, also saw danger signs in Wall Street's innovative financing schemes. In Berkshire Hathaway's *2002 Annual Report to Shareholders,* he specifically noted the perils inherent in derivatives and questioned the complex ways they daisy-chain risk among their counterparties. In summary, he wrote:

---

[54] Dean Baker, *The Run-up in Home Prices: Is It Real or Is It Another Bubble?* (Washington, DC: Center for Economic and Policy Research, 2002) 5.

*Charlie and I are of one mind in how we feel about deriva-
tives and the trading activities that go with them: We view
them as time bombs, both for the parties that deal in them and
the economic system.*[55]

Of course, even Buffet has a less than perfect record on avoiding
risk. The Forbes listing of the world's richest people shows that his
worth declined by $11 billion in just the six months between March
and September 2011, from $50 billion to $39 billion.[56]

One other person who saw trouble brewing was Thomas M. Hoenig,
president of the Federal Reserve Bank of Kansas City. In 1999, at
about the same time that Congress was putting the finishing touches
on the GLBA (thus dismantling the Glass-Steagall Act), Hoenig spoke
before the European Banking and Financial Forum in Czechoslovakia
about the implications of bank "megamergers," such as those between
NationsBank/Bank of America and Citibank/Travelers. He said:

*In a world dominated by megafinancial institutions, govern-
ments could be reluctant to close those that become troubled
for fear of systemic effects on the financial system. To the
extent these institutions become 'too big to fail,' and where
uninsured depositors and other creditors are protected by
implicit government guarantees, the consequences can be
quite serious. Indeed, the result may be a less stable and a
less efficient financial system.* [57]

---

[55] Warren Buffet, *2002 Annual Report* (Omaha, NB: Berkshire Hathaway, Inc.,
    2003) 13.
[56] *Forbes 400: The Richest People in America*, Forbes.com, September 21,
    2011.
[57] Thomas M. Hoenig, Presentation to the European Banking and Financial
    Forum, Prague, March 25, 1999.

Sometimes the American Dream is a Bit More Personal...

Over my thirty-year career with BECU, I've had the great pleasure of working closely with and helping many people. Making a difference in the lives of our members by helping them navigate various life stages to achieve their financial dreams is what I like about working for a credit union. But one of the credit union's richest experiences was helping the Boeing HR manager with a deeply personal dream.

He and his wife were adopting a baby girl, but the cost of adoption was extreme. This man put his faith in us to finance the expense of bringing a child into their life. Our credit union and others were founded on the premise of members helping members. It is a common bond built on personal relationships that brings our community together. This man turned to his credit union for help, and we found a path to the funding he needed for the adoption.

Eighteen years later I hosted a credit union luncheon to award college scholarships. The room was filled with proud parents, but one couple stood out. It was the Boeing HR manager and his wife. Their daughter was now grown, going to college and receiving a scholarship from BECU.

I'm proud to lead an organization that has helped so many people achieve their financial dreams, but one of my fondest memories will always be that scholarship luncheon, and knowing we helped a family complete their dream of adopting a child and sending her to school.

Gary Oakland, President and CEO
Boeing Employees Credit Union

Government Response to the Financial Crisis

Once the magnitude and implications of the financial crisis had become undeniable, the U.S. government promptly stepped in to prevent a total collapse of the domestic and world financial systems. Under the leadership of Treasury Secretary Hank Paulson, a series of rescue plans were quickly formulated with virtually no notice and their details hammered out and revised in weekend-long meetings to reassure markets before they opened on Monday morning. In later interviews, Paulson repeatedly described feeling that he was in a desperate "race" to save the financial system, as new financial calamities seemed to be cropping up on a daily basis.

The initial focus of the government's actions was implementing emergency measures to calm the markets, pump liquidity into the financial system and stem the bleeding. An assortment of different credit facilities and funding programs were created for this purpose – including TARP, the Federal Reserve Rescue Program, and various Federal stimulus programs – ringing up an astounding cumulative tab of more than $3 trillion. While the investment was huge, the emergency measures were viewed as essential by Secretary Paulson, who later remarked, "I hated the things I had to do. It was just much better than the alternative, which was Armageddon." [58]

The second order of business – once the immediate crisis had been averted – was to create a long-term fix to prevent the kinds of risk-taking, lapses in regulatory oversight and credit abuses that turned a spate of mortgage defaults into a global financial tsunami. Congress's endeavor to satisfy this objective culminated in the Dodd-Frank Wall Street Reform and Consumer Protection Act, enacted in July, 2010.

---

[58] Henry Paulson, remarks made during an interview on *The Kudlow Report*, CNBC, February 1, 2010.

Tarp, Federal Rescue Programs & Corporate Bailouts

The various bailout and support programs that were put together by the government and the Fed in the months following the collapse of the housing and CDO markets were among the largest non-defense expenditures ever made.

TARP, the government's most visible program, initially allocated about $700 billion toward the bailout of financial institutions and other businesses that had both caused and been casualties (perhaps we should call them "causeualties") of the financial crisis. [59] Through TARP, the government was able to buy up the unsalable CDOs and other troubled assets on these companies' books, and inject cash into some of the least stable institutions through the purchase of preferred stock and warrants.

The major beneficiaries of TARP included AIG ($70 billion), Chrysler and GM ($77.6 billion), the top 10 banks in the U.S. (just over $165 billion in aggregate), and a large number of smaller financial institutions ($204.7 billion), who were encouraged to take TARP funds.[60] As of August 2011, about half of TARP's total allocation had been invested.

In addition to TARP, some of the other emergency rescue programs put in place to restore the financial system included a $776 billion Treasury program to purchase mortgage-backed securities held by Fannie Mae and Freddie Mac; and a $296 billion Federal Reserve investment in U.S. debt to help keep interest rates down. Billions of additional dollars were also funneled into nearly two dozen smaller programs intended to prevent a complete financial meltdown.

---

[59] This amount was subsequently reduced to about $475 billion by Title XIII of Dodd-Frank bill, known as the "Pay It Back Act."

[60] It is noteworthy that TARP funds and other forms of relief were not made available to the nation's credit unions at the time – showing how government is often tone-deaf to the needs of smaller financial institutions.

Figure 16 - Financial Crisis Bailout Tracker, 2009
($ Billions)[61]

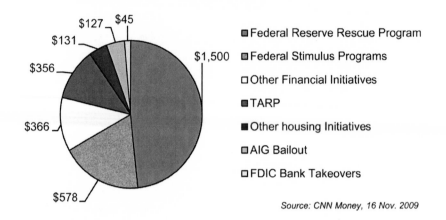

$127 $45
$131
$356
$366
$578
$1,500

◼ Federal Reserve Rescue Program

◻ Federal Stimulus Programs

◻ Other Financial Initiatives

◼ TARP

◼ Other housing Initiatives

◻ AIG Bailout

◻ FDIC Bank Takeovers

Source: CNN Money, 16 Nov. 2009

It is worth noting that, in addition to providing the resources to save our financial system, TARP provided a convenient repository for wasteful "pork" programs championed by a rogue's gallery of lobbyists and policymakers. These included such items as an exemption from excise tax for toy wooden arrows, a favorable cost recovery plan for an automobile race track, incentives for adult films shot in the United States, coverage of bicycle repair as an employee benefit for bike commuters, and a suspension of duties on wool products. This kind of opportunism at a time of national crisis exposed one the great weaknesses in our political system and exacerbated a growing lack of public confidence in its legislative leadership.

On the other side of the coin, much of the funding the government provided to the largest financial institutions during the financial crisis has now been paid back – plus dividends, interest and warrants, which in some cases provided a substantial profit to the U.S. taxpayer. According to data from Bloomberg, the government earned $22.89 billion from the ten most profitable TARP repayments to date, which

---

[61] U.S. Federal Reserve, U.S Treasury, FDIC, Congressional Budget Office, and The White House in *CNN Money*, November 16, 2009: http://money.cnn. com/news/storysupplement/economy/bailouttracker.

included Bank of America, Citigroup, GMAC Financial, Goldman Sachs, Hartford Financial, JPMorgan Chase, Morgan Stanley, PNC Financial Services, SunTrust Banks and Wells Fargo.[62] Of this group, all but Citigroup, GMAC and Suntrust have paid the government back in full.

The U.S. taxpayer has also received approximately $9 billion to date from the sale and repurchase of warrants that the government acquired from TARP participants.[63] What is interesting to me is that the banks who paid back their TARP funds are the ones that are meticulously eviscerated in the press, while the other folks who took money and did not pay it back, including Fannie and Freddie, hardly ever get mentioned.

The Dodd-Frank Wall Street Reform and Consumer Protection Act

If we view TARP as the government's reactive response to the financial crisis, then Dodd-Frank was intended to be its proactive cousin. The most sweeping overhaul to the U.S. financial regulation since the Glass-Steagall reforms of the 1930s, the 2,319-page Dodd-Frank Act was signed into law in 2010 "to promote the financial stability of the United States by improving accountability and transparency in the financial system, to end 'Too Big to Fail,' to protect the American taxpayer by ending bailouts, to protect consumers from abusive financial services practices, and for other purposes."[64]

---

[62] "The Treasury: Making Money on the Bank Bailout," *Bloomberg Businessweek*, October 25, 2010.
[63] U.S. Treasury. "Monthly 105(a) Report," August 2011.
[64] Dodd-Frank Wall Street Reform and Consumer Protection Act, Pub. L. no. 111-203, 124 Stat 1376 (2010).

The Hidden Cost of TARP Funds for Smaller Institutions

Although America's largest banks were required to participate in the TARP program, a number of smaller community banks also chose to participate, as did certain non-bank entities such as AIG, Fannie Mae and Freddie Mac.

Why were these smaller banks willing to accept TARP funds? The primary impetus was the notion that TARP represented access to low-cost capital. Since most banks' stock prices were undervalued during the crisis, raising capital through stock issuance would have proved costly. Instead, a bank could use TARP funds to boost its capital ratios and pay only 5% per year for the first five years. Many banks saw this as an attractive way to raise capital and fund growth.

But accepting TARP funds had other "hidden" costs, which led most banks to eschew TARP funding. First, the reporting requirements were not well defined (and eventually proved to be highly burdensome). Second, participation in TARP effectively resulted in the federal government becoming a shareholder of the bank, albeit through non-voting shares. Wary U.S. bankers recalled how Britain had implemented a program similar to TARP that was considered to have nationalized the British banking industry.

Second, TARP restricted the ways that participating banks could pay dividends and compensate employees. For example, new executives could not be given "golden parachutes." Executive compensation was also limited to a $500,000 maximum tax deduction per executive. These provisions limited the ability of a bank to attract top talent and also effectively increased the cost of the program, due to the tax impact.

(continued on next page)

Perhaps most important, many banks were concerned about the public relations impact of accepting TARP funds. The banking industry was viewed by many as the catalyst of the financial crisis, and TARP was viewed as a bailout to those that had caused the problem. In retrospect, it seems apparent that this last concern was well-founded. While the banking industry has repaid over 90% of its TARP funding, it still has not escaped the stigma of TARP. Those financial institutions that chose not to accept TARP funds have been able to market themselves as TARP-free. Many have seen growth as a result of this decision, as consumers not only objected to the notion of bail-outs, but also viewed those institutions that accepted TARP funds as less stable institutions.

Bill Handel, Vice President of Research
Raddon Financial Group

★ ★ ★

Put simply, Dodd-Frank was designed to repair the glaring weaknesses that were exposed during the financial crisis and try to prevent a repeat performance. While this may seem like closing the barn door after the horse has bolted, it was at least a step in the right direction. The legislation that emerged touches nearly every corner of the financial landscape – Wall Street, banking, credit ratings agencies, mortgage lenders and consumers. According to *American Banker*, the Act is expected to add 2,847 new staff to government agencies and receive $1.25 billion in funding between 2010 and 2012.[65]

Dodd-Frank did away with or consolidated the responsibilities of numerous regulatory agencies, some of whose powers and organization had proven ineffective before and during the crisis. At the same time,

---

[65]   Government Accounting Office, in Glen Fest, "The Dodd-Frank Effect," *American Banker Magazine*, November 2011: 21.

it established a 15-member Financial Stability Oversight Council to monitor and evaluate institutions and remedy situations that could pose a systemic risk.

To avoid the kind of haphazard bank closures that occurred during the financial crisis, Dodd-Frank provided a general blueprint for dealing with future crises – including clear processes for winding-down or liquidating bankrupt firms.

Dodd-Frank also introduced a smorgasbord of new regulations to the financial markets, including several aimed at regulating derivatives. To make derivative-based risk exposure more obvious, the bill will require trading many derivatives on exchanges, rather than allowing them to be signed, sealed and delivered in the secrecy of corporate suites.

Reviving the spirit of the Glass-Steagall Act, the bill introduced the "Volcker Rule," which limits (but does not entirely prevent) the ability of depository banks to engage in proprietary trading, such as the private hedge fund operations that put many banks in trouble during the crisis.

Dodd-Frank also introduced major changes to bank capital ratios. The Collins Amendment to the Dodd-Frank Act increased capital requirements for financial institutions generally, while disallowing certain types of capital (such as trust preferred securities) from Tier 1 capital calculations altogether. This will effectively force banks to find new sources of replacement capital. In addition, a section of the Volcker Rule requires regulators to impose "countercyclical" capital requirements upon institutions, such that greater amounts of capital are required in times of economic expansion and reduced amounts in times of economic contraction.

A variety of mortgage lending reforms were introduced by Dodd-Frank in direct response to the sub-prime disaster. These reforms put stricter underwriting requirements in place to eliminate low-documentation and no-documentation loans, eliminate "steering incentives" that target specific neighborhoods, and create guidelines to help ensure that borrowers are reasonably able to repay their loans.

The bill also introduced a spate of consumer-focused reforms, placing them under the direction of a newly created Consumer Financial Protection Bureau (CFPB). The CFPB is broadly tasked with prohibiting unfair, deceptive or abusive practices, and ensuring that adequate disclosures are provided to consumers of financial services.

By some counts, the Dodd-Frank Act mandated nearly 400 new rules for the financial industry to comply with...and there is the prospect of even more rules to come as the CFPB begins to clarify and define its regulatory role. That said, Dodd-Frank is still very much a work in progress, and the influence of powerful lobbying groups makes it likely that whatever emerges will be a watered-down, lopsided version of what was originally envisioned. As of this writing:[66]

- 38 rules have been finalized

- 26 rule deadlines have been missed

- 121 rules have been proposed

- 215 rules have future deadlines

- 87 studies have been required, of which 35 have been completed and 2 deadlines missed

---

[66] Davis Polk & Wardwell LLP, *Dodd-Frank Progress Report*, July 2011.

- Critical SEC and Commodity Futures Trading Commission (CFTC) programs mandated by the act have not received funding

- Major provisions, such as the Volcker Rule, are still under discussion and may not be passed

What could not be addressed by Dodd-Frank – or by any other piece of legislation – was the widespread culture of entitlement in American society that was as much to blame for the crisis as any other ingredient. Flipping homes, double mortgages, living beyond one's means, and taking on unreasonable amounts of debt are weaknesses that no piece of legislation can mask.

The Unintended Consequences of Financial Reform

Intelligent people can disagree about the specific steps that the U.S. took in response to the financial crisis, from TARP to Dodd-Frank and the Durbin Amendment. I personally believe that – as painful as these steps were – the course of action America took was essential to protect the world's financial systems, and I credit our leaders for acting swiftly and decisively. To appreciate the hazards of indecision and inaction, one only needs to look at the repercussions of the 2011 U.S. debt ceiling negotiations or the sovereign debt contagion that is spreading throughout Europe.

I also think it would be a mistake to lay the blame for the financial crisis entirely upon the large investment banks or mortgage lenders. As many observers have noted, there was plenty of blame to go around – from government housing and interest rate policies to predatory lenders and opportunistic home buyers; from Wall Street bankers and greedy investors to cursory due diligence by credit ratings agencies.

While it is true that the large banks had a disproportionate role in the financial crisis, they also paid the dearest price (in paybacks and warrants), as did investors who sought short-term profits from the crisis and wound up with huge losses. Other parties, such as GM, have not yet fully repaid their obligations, and the problems at Fannie and Freddie remain unresolved.

Moreover, the U.S. government has consistently failed to acknowledge its own role in creating a policy landscape that all but guaranteed that the financial crisis would occur, through the Fed's loose monetary policy, the unrestrained activities of Fannie Mae and Freddie Mac, the Community Reinvestment Act and Gramm-Leach-Bliley.

It has often been the case that policies put in place for one reason have repercussions extending into unexpected and unintended areas. And sometimes, the harm caused by such unintended consequences far outweighs the good that the policy was designed to produce.

The U.S. Prohibition laws of the 1920s are an obvious example of such unintended consequences. Originally designed to curb the social evils associated with alcohol consumption, the Prohibition laws ended up supporting another kind of evil that proved far worse: organized crime. Because the Prohibition laws banned the legal distribution of alcohol, they gave rise to a widespread and highly profitable black market controlled by mobs in organized crime. The mobs then used the money derived from their alcohol trade to finance endeavors in bookmaking, prostitution, and other nefarious enterprises.

A more recent example of unintended policy consequences was a provision in the Patient Protection and Affordable Care Act (PPACA) of 2010. One small detail in the Act – which had nothing to do with the bill's primary purpose – required businesses to issue 1099 tax forms to all vendors paid more than $600 per year. What the government failed to realize was that, by including this minor provision, it was placing a major compliance burden on small businesses all across America. After the enormity of this unintended consequence became apparent, the provision was wisely repealed.

The No Child Left Behind mandate of 2001, which sought to improve educational performance in America's public schools, also had important unintended consequences. Because the mandate tied federal funding to improvements in overall performance levels at schools, it had the effect of shifting school resources and attention toward students with the lowest scores in reading and mathematics. The unintended consequence was that this came at the expense of programs designed for advanced and gifted students, and left that group increasingly underfunded and underserved.

The financial reform policies of TARP and Dodd-Frank are no different from these examples. In seeking to de-risk the banking industry, stabilize the economy and protect the consumer, we have introduced policies that are seriously undermining all of these areas. These policies, which were designed to shore up America's large capital markets banks, have made it harder for consumers and businesses to obtain credit, strangled job growth, and put significant and undue strains on our smaller Main Street banks that played almost no role in the financial crisis.

Henry Hazlitt, an influential 20th century American economist, once observed that the fatal flaw in nearly all economic policies was their failure to anticipate long-term consequences and account for all possible outcomes. He said: "The art of economics consists in looking not merely at the immediate but at the longer effects of any act or policy; it consists in tracing the consequences of that policy not merely for one group but for all groups."[67]

---

[67] Henry Hazlitt, *Economics in One Lesson* (New York: Harper & Brothers, 1946) 2.

We are now in the position where we have succeeded in saving America's largest banks – even allowing them to generate record earnings, add to their accounts and assets, and lower their costs of capital. But by failing to anticipate the consequences of the policies that made this recovery possible, we have simultaneously endangered our nation's ranks of smaller community banks and credit unions, which entered the financial crisis stronger and emerged far weaker than the large banks did.

Over the past several years, I have met with the leaders of community-based financial institutions all across America and around the world. Time and time again, they tell me that the government simply doesn't understand them; that they are being inundated by policies and regulations that are out of step with their operational realities and contrary to the best interests of the communities they serve.

Solving one problem without creating another, or helping one group without harming another is a perennial challenge in creating policy. By this measure, I believe our current financial reform policies are a complete failure. They are certain to hasten the erosion of our valuable community banks and credit unions while making it harder for the ones that remain to do what they do best, which is lubricating and supporting the economies of America's communities. After all, what is our national economy, if not the sum total of thousands of individual community economies?

Why Community-Based Financial Institutions Matter

Community-based financial institutions are America's "Main Street" financial institutions. They consist of banks and credit unions that are relatively small in size (under $10 billion in assets) and do most of their business in the communities in which they are located. In the case of credit unions, they may even be restricted to serving only a certain group of people within a highly specific geography. In general, community-based financial institutions focus on offering essential financial services (such as basic checking and savings accounts, mortgages, and personal, small business and commercial real-estate loans). They derive their strength from the close, long-term relationships they maintain with the people in their communities and the deep knowledge they possess about their local economies.

Nearly all community-based financial institutions began as firms that were locally owned, staffed and operated. They make lending decisions locally, based on personal knowledge of their customers and members. They invest in their communities not only through lending, but also by playing an active role in community affairs and supporting the organizations that benefit the neighborhoods where they do business.

Making and Keeping Promises...

In 2010, the leadership team at Vermont State Employees Credit Union developed a brand promise: *We are a banking co-op dedicated to improving the quality of life for all Vermonters.* The promise hangs in our board room to guide key business decisions and it was a critical part of our disaster recovery plan in the summer of 2011.

As Hurricane Irene battered Vermont with severe flooding, my executive leadership team worked through the night tracking the storm. When dawn broke, we saw that river banks around the state had swallowed roads and homes. The Winooski River overflowed and devastated our Waterbury branch.

With their homes destroyed and lives in turmoil, Vermonters focused on recovery and needed money to buy food, supplies, clothes and other necessities. But our local branch was gone.

(continued on next page)

Working with the Vermont Association of Credit Unions and others, I called recreational vehicle companies from Vermont to Texas, scouring the country for an RV that could become a full-service credit union on wheels. I found one in Indiana, equipped with a secure vault, satellite service for ATM transactions and systems that allowed us to operate laptop computers. It had two teller stations and a small manager's office in an enclosed area behind the steering wheel.

The space was cramped. Our staff literally rubbed elbows with our members. But the intimacy comforted people. It encouraged them to share their stories. We listened, not as their banker or credit union, but as their neighbor. Parked on a quiet street in Waterbury, we continued serving our members in the storm's aftermath - fulfilling our brand promise in a rented RV from Indiana.

Steven D. Post, CEO
Vermont State Employees Credit Union

In a very real sense, community banks and credit unions help to support the American Dream by helping people to reinvest in their own communities. Their role is memorably depicted in the 1946 Frank Capra movie, *It's a Wonderful Life,* when the film's main character, George Bailey (played by Jimmy Stewart) explains to a mob of angry townspeople making a run on their local bank why the bank can't return their money:

> *The money's not here. Well, your money's in Joe's house...*
> *that's right next to yours. And in the Kennedy house, and Mrs.*
> *Macklin's house, and, and a hundred others. Why, you're*
> *lending them the money to build, and then, they're going to*

pay it back to you as best they can. Now what are you going to do? Foreclose on them?[68]

Despite their small size and humble origins, community-based financial institutions are a potent force in the U.S. economy. They represent 92% of all banks in America.[69] Taken as a group, they would be the largest financial institution in the country. While they hold only about 24% of U.S. bank assets, community-based financial institutions provide 58% of all loans to small businesses – in other words, they disproportionately support the firms that constitute 99.7% of all employer firms in America and accounted for 65% of the 15 million net new jobs created between 1993 and 2009.[70]

Community-based financial institutions also support the families whose consumption drives more than 70% of the U.S. GDP.[71] They provide a disproportionate share of all home mortgages, hold their own mortgage paper, and carry most of their loans to maturity (which is one reason why they largely sidestepped the sub-prime mortgage crisis). And because they maintain a vested interest in the performance of their loans, they enjoy lower delinquency and charge-off rates as a group compared to larger institutions.

Their community-oriented business focus, prudent financial practices, and intimate knowledge of their account holders and local economies make community-based financial institutions the true engine of America's prosperity. They are intimately tied to every single tenet of the American Dream; they are the financial intermediaries that make

---

[68] *It's A Wonderful Life*, dir. Frank Capra, perf. James Stewart, Liberty Films (II), 1946.

[69] FDIC, 2011.

[70] Independent Community Bankers of America, *Community Banking Facts*, September 2011.

[71] The World Bank, "United States Household Final Consumption Expenditure % of GDP," *World Development Indicators*, 2009: http://data.worldbank.org/indicator/NE.CON.PETC.ZS.

it possible to own a home, run a business, get an education, save for retirement, buy a car, take a vacation, and protect one's savings.

Figure 17 - Market Share of Top Five Banks vs. Smaller Banks, 2010

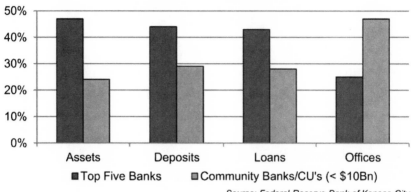

Source: Federal Reserve Bank of Kansas City

Community banks and credit unions stand in contrast to America's largest banks, the top 10 of which control 47% of all U.S. bank deposits.[72] The large banks' business model is built around meeting the capital needs of large enterprises and wealthy customers, and satisfying the expectations of their shareholders. In recent years, large bank profits have been driven more by their investments in capital markets than by lending.

Because of their different business model, large banks are not especially focused on meeting the needs of small retail customers. Their credit decisions for such customers are more likely to be dictated by corporate guidelines and FICO credit scores rather than individual knowledge and relationships. In addition, a mortgage loan from a large bank is usually resold to a third-party, with the resulting funds likely to be channeled into projects outside the immediate community.

---

[72] FDIC, June 30, 2010.

Although some community-based financial institutions did make bad decisions and mistakes in the period leading up to the financial crisis, they were not a significant factor in sub-prime lending or the derivatives markets. Nevertheless, the fallout from the financial crisis has made these cornerstones of community life an endangered species. The credit market freeze and caution that followed the financial crisis did not discriminate between large and small banks; it damaged the reputations and lending ability of all banks, causing many community-based financial institutions to undergo voluntary and forced consolidations, and prompted a staggering number of bank closures.

Prior to the financial crisis, community-based financial institutions experienced relatively few failures…and the failures that did occur among community banks were more than made up for by a healthy number of new bank charters. But since 2009, this trend has been completely inverted. From 2009 to August 2011, there were 373 FDIC-insured community bank failures and just 43 new bank charters, amounting to a large decline in the overall number of institutions.[73] Worse yet, the list of bank failures continues to grow larger each year while the number of "de novo" (new) bank applications continues to shrink.

Figure 18 - Newly Formed FDIC Insured Institutions, 2001-2010

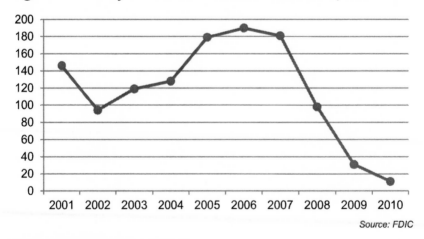

Source: FDIC

---

[73] FDIC, August 2011.

Credit unions, which serve approximately 90 million Americans, were also badly damaged by the financial crisis. While the number of credit union closures was small in comparison to community bank closures, that is because credit unions typically don't just close up shop. In a spirit of "taking care of their own," most troubled credit unions end up merging with stronger credit unions to continue serving the institution's members. Nevertheless, in just the four years from 2007 through 2010, there were a total of 85 credit union liquidations and involuntary mergers, 890 voluntary mergers, and only 13 new credit union charters.[74] This continues a long-term trend of declines in the total number of credit unions.

Adding to the challenges in an industry that takes care of its own, the remaining credit unions are also paying the price for a spate of ill-advised investments in mortgage-backed securities made by a handful of "corporate" credit unions just prior to the financial crisis. These corporate credit unions – which provide vital correspondent banking, liquidity, and investment services to consumer credit unions – suffered huge losses from their investments and were eventually taken over by the National Credit Union Association. The outcome of this is that all credit unions are now required by the NCUA to make payments for ten years into an insurance fund to help clean up the mess and make good on the losses of these few institutions. This decade-long stream of payments – the amounts of which are considerable – not only diverts funds that could otherwise be used to serve members, but will also threaten the profitability and survival of many credit unions in the future.

---

[74] National Credit Union Association, Annual Reports, 2007-2010.

Public Policy, Regulatory Changes and their Chilling Effect

The collapse of many large U.S. financial institutions has led to numerous new regulatory burdens for all U.S. financial institutions and many of these policy changes are ultimately hurting consumers. In an effort aimed at restraining the mismanagement practices of these financial mega giants, Congress has unthinkingly placed additional burdens on well-run credit unions and smaller banks.

Regulatory changes with short deadlines, fee restrictions and added bureaucratic expenses have caused many credit unions to delay projects that might otherwise benefit our members. Financial institutions have also had to invest in additional tools to monitor compliance with the new regulations. Much of this has forced financial institutions to impose new fees and restructure otherwise free products to offset lost income and additional compliance costs.

Here are some of the more glaring examples of how public policy has caused lost efficiencies and increased expenses to credit unions, and consumers:

Dodd-Frank Act: Home Ownership Equity Protection Act (HOEPA) requires financial institutions to track the average prime offer rate on a weekly basis. Unfortunately, the added work of weekly tracking and rate comparison does not provide any benefit to consumers.

Dodd-Frank also requires significant disclosures and fee changes related to credit cards. Fee reductions do not help average consumers. Fee reductions, however, benefit borrowers who do not pay their credit card bills on time.

(continued on next page)

The Good Faith Mortgage Estimate document was revised from a 1-page document to a 3-page document. While the intent of this document is to protect borrowers from fee-related surprises at closing, the regulation is too complex to meet this objective and will not benefit consumers.

The Consumer Financial Protection Bureau (CFPB) has also been added to the government bureaucracy. The CFPB may build a whole new set of regulations which adds to uncertainty, creates risk in the market and, I believe, will ultimately raise prices on loans. Uncertainty and excessive oversight has also caused many financial institutions to deny credit to worthy borrowers.

I'm all for protecting and adequately informing consumers. I agree that there existed a need to reform some questionable practices in the financial services industry, especially at the largest mega institutions. But what has occurred is an overkill that punishes the innocent who have always looked out for Main Street's best interest without regulatory mandates. It would be hard to find hidden fees or tricky interest rate increases at credit unions. What you will find is free, broad and effective financial education for our members.

Lary B. McCants, CCD, CCE, Chairman
Credit Union Executives Society

Of course, large banks had troubles during the crisis, too, and those that stayed late at the party did not survive the hangover. The banking giants Wachovia and Washington Mutual both collapsed under the weight of their sub-prime mortgages. Still, government support and rescue funds helped to make the five largest U.S. financial institutions

20% larger after the crisis than they were beforehand.[75] Meanwhile, community banks and credit unions emerged in worse shape than ever. They were either left to fend for themselves or, if they accepted TARP funds, they were burdened with meeting reporting and repayment terms that were inconsistent with the capital and operational resources of smaller institutions.

All of this is not to say that large banks are inherently bad and that small banks are inherently good. Each type of institution plays an important role in society and in America's economic life. But while some people may argue about the fairness of bailing out the larger banks, few people would dispute the inequity of helping out the larger banks in a way that punished the smaller ones.

As I said earlier, our community banks and credit unions entered the financial crisis among the strongest financial institutions in the country. They had higher capital ratios, lower loan-loss provisions, fewer charged off loans and far less exposure to sub-prime lending than larger banks. Today, however, we have raised the bar on what it costs to establish and run a bank or credit union. As a result, many once-strong community-based financial institutions are literally struggling to survive as a consequence of the abuses of large institutions and the reforms that followed. When we consider how essential community-based financial institutions are to our local economies (and by extension, the national economy), it is clear that we must end the needless harm and instead offer the support needed to continue fulfilling their important role in the future.

---

[75] Neil M. Barofsky, "Where the Bailout Went Wrong," *New York Times*, March 29, 2011.

Consumers Prefer Community Banks and Credit Unions

I have discussed the role that community-based financial institutions play in maintaining healthy communities, ensuring a healthy economy, and preserving a sustainable American dream. But you may be wondering whether community bank customers and credit union members place a similarly high value on these characteristics.

Research from the Raddon Financial Group indicates that they do. The firm, which conducts nationwide consumer and small business surveys on banking preferences, has tracked attitudes toward banking relationships for nearly 30 years. In their most recent survey, small businesses confirmed a higher-than-average level of satisfaction with community-based financial institutions (45% satisfied) than with a top-five bank (32% satisfied).[76]

Figure 19 - Small Business Satisfaction with Financial Institutions, 2011

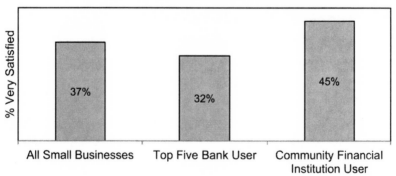

Source: Raddon Financial Group

Furthermore, 48% of small businesses using a top-five bank indicated that access to credit seemed to have dried up – probably because of the

---

[76] Raddon Financial Group, *Fall 2011 National Small Business Survey*, October 2011.

strict rules that govern big banks' lending programs.[77] Historically, big banks tighten these rules even further in response to economic and regulatory pressures, which means they provide less support for consumers and small businesses at the times when they need it most.

Figure 20 - Small Business Perception of Credit Availability, 2011

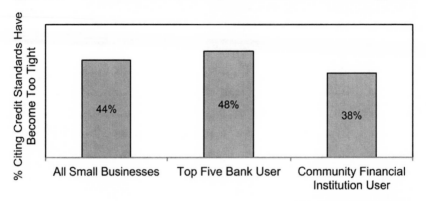

Source: Raddon Financial Group

Consumers generally preferred community-based financial institutions, as well. Regardless of whether they used a large bank or a small bank or credit union as their primary financial institution, 57% of all consumers surveyed by Raddon agreed that smaller institutions offer more personalized service, while only 10% disagreed with that statement.[78]

Consumers using small institutions were also twice as likely to rate their bank or credit union as "extremely or somewhat supportive" (32%) during the recent economic downturn versus "not at all or not very supportive" (17%). Meanwhile, large bank users were almost equally split, with 24% labeling their bank "not at all or not very

---

[77] Ibid.
[78] Raddon Financial Group, *Fall 2011 National Consumer Survey*, October 2011.

supportive" versus 26% saying it was "extremely or somewhat supportive."[79]

Raddon's research also uncovered an area of universal agreement concerning large banks, and that is concern about the TARP bailouts. Over half of all households surveyed by Raddon said they were less likely to use a big bank because of the bailouts. The sentiment was strongest among non-big-five users, 59% of whom said they shared this opinion. Even more interesting, 47% of those who currently use a large bank agreed with the statement.[80] There clearly remains a lot of worry over the bailouts that may affect future consumer banking decisions.

Figure 21 - Consumer Sentiment Toward Bank Bailouts, 2011

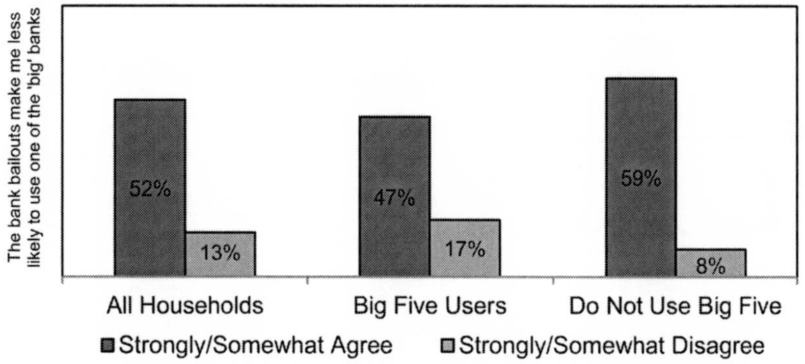

Source: Raddon Financial Group

The Impact of Reform on Community-Based Institutions

A news reporter recently asked me if I thought the large banks and the government were engaged in a conspiracy to eliminate the

---

[79] Raddon Financial Group, *Spring 2011 National Consumer Survey*, March 2011.
[80] Raddon Financial Group, *Fall 2011 National Consumer Survey*, October 2011.

community banks through policies like TARP, Dodd-Frank and the Durbin Amendment. I said that I didn't think there was a conspiracy; but if there were one, it was working.[81]

Dodd-Frank is a blunt instrument that will inject massive amounts of government red tape into the banking system as a whole. Like the credit freeze, the Act does not do a good job of discriminating between large and small banks and, for this reason, it has the potential to further undermine the American Dream. Although most of the Dodd-Frank regulations were intended to curb the irresponsible practices of large banks, lenders, insurance companies and investment firms, the burden of compliance will affect all financial institutions and fall especially hard on small community banks and credit unions.

Some particularly significant areas in which Dodd-Frank has produced unintended negative consequences for community-based financial institutions are in the areas of compliance, fee income, capital access, and capital funding standards.

Increased Compliance Costs

It is hard to put an exact figure on the compliance costs associated with Dodd-Frank because so many details of the Act's rules and processes have yet to be spelled out. But based on the rules that are in place, some experts estimate that compliance with the Act will result in 2,260,631 labor hours and approximately $866 million in direct costs for the financial industry.[82]

Whatever the actual figures turn out to be, there is no doubt that Dodd-Frank compliance will take a major bite out of financial institution

---

[81] "Taking Stock," *Bloomberg Radio*, September 8, 2011.
[82] For labor hours, see: Rep. Sean Duffy, "Dodd-Frank: One Year Later," *Washington Times*, July 20, 2011. For direct costs, see: Sam Batkins, "The costs of Dodd-Frank? Even the Feds don't know," *The Hill Congressional Blog*, May 18, 2011.

profits for the foreseeable future and become one of the major costs of running a bank or credit union.

Banks of all types will need to design, develop, populate and review a raft of compliance-related reporting systems. Small banks, in particular, will need to hire full-time compliance officers and possibly additional compliance personnel. Part-time compliance supervision will no longer be enough.

Large banks are in a better position to weather the added compliance requirements because of their larger IT and compliance staffs and greater financial resources. Small banks will find the costs much harder to bear, with fewer sources of income. As the Chairman-elect of the American Bankers Association noted in congressional testimony on the compliance cost of Dodd-Frank, "Historically, the cost of regulatory compliance as a share of operating expenses is two-and-a-half times greater for small banks than for large banks."[83] And bear in mind that the increased attention to compliance means time away from the customer relationships that are the key source of strength for smaller financial institutions.

The requirements of increased Federal regulation and the costs of compliance have become so burdensome that they have forced at least some community financial institutions to exit banking altogether. For instance, the 27-year-old Main Street Bank in Kingwood, Texas surrendered its banking charter and sold its four branches to a nearby bank in 2011 after regulators demanded that the bank increase its capital ratios, strengthen its financial controls, change its lending practices and replace its CEO.[84]

---

[83] Albert C. Kelley, Jr., Testimony at the House Subcommittee on Financial Institutions and Consumer Credit, *The Effect of Dodd-Frank on Small Financial Institutions and Small Businesses*, March 2, 2011.

[84] Robin Sidel, "Fed Up: A Texas Bank Is Calling It Quits," *Wall Street Journal*, August 10, 2011.

Another bank, Teche Holding Co. of New Iberia, Louisiana, switched from being a federally chartered thrift to a state bank in a move that it anticipated would reduce its federal regulatory fees by $100,000 per year. In a press release, Teche Bank's CEO, Patrick Little, said that Dodd-Frank had effectively eliminated the advantages of a federal savings bank charter.[85]

Reduced Income that Threatens Services

Limiting fee income is one of the most critical areas where Dodd-Frank and other reform policies have had unintended negative consequences for small banks and credit unions. In the long run, fee-income policies designed to save consumers money are one of the areas where the policy may actually end up costing them more.

All banks and credit unions rely on non-interest fee income to offset costs in other areas, from operational costs (including compliance) to services such as free checking, online bill payment, and mobile banking. Non-interest fee income is also what makes it possible for community banks and credit unions to provide the high service levels that their customers and members enjoy. This fee income stems from sources such as overdraft fees, deposit and transaction fees, and debit card "swipe" fees – the interchange fees that merchants pay when a customer uses the financial institution's debit card.

A regulation issued by the Federal Reserve in 2010, known as Regulation E, limits the fee income that banks may collect, supposedly to protect consumers from "hidden" charges, despite the fact that the associated charges are spelled out in every customer account agreement. Regulation E prohibits financial institutions from charging for overdrafts on ATM and one-time debit card transactions, unless the consumer "opts-in" and agrees to be charged for such transactions. The

---

[85] Teche Holding Company, *Teche Holding Company Announces Completion of Teche Federal Bank Charter Conversion*, June 22, 2011.

Boston Consulting Group, among others, has estimated that Regulation E will deliver a $12 to $15 billion hit to banks' fee income per year.[86]

More recently, the Durbin Amendment to Dodd-Frank gave the Federal Reserve the right to set limits on debit card swipe fees. The Fed has currently capped these fees at 21 cents plus 0.05% of the transaction (with the possibility of earning an additional cent under certain circumstances). Prior to the Fed action, swipe fees earned about 44 cents per transaction, which means the Fed cut this source of fee income by more than half.

While the Fed action was intended to bring bank fees more in line with actual costs, the final amount it settled upon does not reflect many of the hidden costs associated with swipe fees, including costs for things like fraud prevention, loss reserves, and other operational risks. The Durbin Amendment was also somewhat unfair to banks in the sense that it shifted profits on swipe fees from banks to retailers. While Durbin presumed that consumers would benefit from lower prices as a result of the lower swipe fees, in fact most retailers are simply pocketing the savings, rather than passing them along to the consumer. I believe it is no coincidence that Wal-Mart and other retailers had an inordinate influence on the final legislation by donating tens of millions of dollars to the amendment's leading backers and programs benefiting their constituents.[87]

Although financial institutions with less than $10 billion in assets are technically exempted from the Fed's cap on swipe fees, in practice the small banks will have to match the 21-cent interchange fee to remain competitive with larger banks. It has been estimated that this

[86] Andy Maguire et al., "Global Retail Banking 2010/2011: The Road to Excellence," The Boston Consulting Group, bcg.perspectives, December 14, 2010.

[87] Marcus Rothaar, "So Bank of America, How's the Water?" *Raddon Report*, October 13, 2011.

will cost community banks and credit unions another several billion dollars in lost fee revenue.

Why is this so unfair to smaller institutions? Because for large banks, non-interest fee income is just one source of revenue that can be used to offset other costs. Large banks may earn fees from selling insurance and investment products, and from investment banking activities such as underwriting public stock offerings. Because of their scale, they also enjoy a lower cost structure per customer and can earn more from relatively small fee increases in high volume transaction areas. But community-based financial institutions are hard-pressed to find ways of making up for lost fee income. They have a traditional product set and low margins. They must rely on operational efficiency and higher quality loans to subsidize services like free checking.

By limiting the amounts that banks and credit unions can collect from debit card transactions, overdrafts and other areas, Regulation E and the Durbin Amendment force smaller institutions to charge new or higher fees for existing services, such as checking accounts, or reduce services to the underserved. The hallmark of credit unions, for instance, is serving the underserved and providing less well-off members with access to the same services enjoyed by those with greater means. Faced with rising costs and few options to offset these expenses, no access to capital other than through retained earnings, and restrictions on areas like business lending, it's no wonder that 975 credit unions either closed or merged with other credit unions in the four years from 2007 through 2010.[88]

This not only places community-based financial institutions at a distinct competitive disadvantage, but also directly hurts consumers and small businesses. We have already seen that large banks were among the first to charge fees for debit card usage and slash their free

---

[88] National Credit Union Association, Annual Reports, 2007-2010.

checking accounts to offset reduced fee income. But smaller banks are hard-pressed to do the same, since free checking is one of the few basic services they offer.

Higher Capital and Fewer Ways to Get It

Another policy with unintended consequences for smaller financial institutions is the Collins Amendment to the Dodd-Frank Act. After the financial crisis made it clear that some banks had maintained inadequate capital levels relative to their risk exposure, the Collins Amendment mandated higher and more stringent capital requirements for all banks. Although the exact capital levels have yet to be finalized, the Collins Amendment has already made clear that it will limit what qualifies as bank capital to include little more than shareholder interest and retained earnings.

Of particular concern to community-based financial institutions is that the Collins Amendment no longer permits newly issued Trust Preferred Securities (TRUPS) – a long-term, debt-based issue favored by bank holding companies – to be included in Tier 1 capital. The significance of this change was highlighted by Camden Fine, President and CEO of the Independent Community Bankers of America, in a letter to Congress:

> The inclusion of TRUPS in Tier 1 capital has long been allowed by regulators, subject to limitations. Community banks in particular, with few practical options for raising capital, have relied on TRUPS. An abrupt change in the rules would cause hundreds of community banks to become capital deficient and force them to reduce lending in order to restore their capital ratios.[89]

---

[89] Camden R. Fine, Letter from the ICBA to Chairman Barney Frank and Ranking Member Spencer Bachus of the Committee on Financial Services, June 10, 2010.

It goes without saying that community-based financial institutions have a hard time raising capital in any environment. Large banks, like Bank of America and Goldman Sachs, can attract large cash infusions from Warren Buffet, while Citigroup can raise money from sovereign wealth funds in China and the Middle East. But there is no parallel capability for community banks, which must rely on private investors to raise capital, or for credit unions, which have no source beyond retained earnings for raising capital.

The Collins Amendment just makes raising capital that much more challenging for smaller institutions. So does a change in the definition of an "Accredited Investor" initiated by Dodd-Frank, which no longer allows private investors to include the value of their primary residence when calculating net worth. This effectively raises the $1 million threshold that private investors must meet and reduces the number of people eligible to provide capital to smaller banks. Community-based financial institutions have a long history of being funded by wealthy individuals in the community, particularly when larger institutions have failed to serve their needs. Raising the bar for qualified investors simply cuts off important sources of capital and makes it harder to serve our communities' financial needs.

While the issues involved can get fairly technical, the main points to take away from the capital access policies are fairly simple. The first is that raising overall capital ratios and changing what qualifies as capital disproportionately harms smaller financial institutions because they have fewer options for raising capital than larger banks do. The second point is that any money devoted to bank capital reserves is money not being used for a more productive purpose, such as lending. And this doesn't just make it harder for smaller financial institutions to do what they do best; it also hurts the American economy.

The Real Threat to the American Dream

Throughout this chapter, I've discussed how recent policies and trends are crippling the community-based financial institutions that play such an important role in supporting the tenets of the American Dream. The question now is what will happen if these policies and trends continue.

Faced with huge regulatory compliance costs, credit standards that make it hard for them to do business, reduced fee income and increased capital requirements, many of our community banks and credit unions could find they have no alternative but to consolidate with each other, become absorbed into a larger bank, or simply close their doors and call it a day.

The small community-based financial institutions that remain would be forced to charge higher fees or reduce services to make up for their higher costs of doing business, which means they would be less able to meet community needs or contribute to community programs.

If only large banks survive, families and small businesses would probably find less choice in the programs and services available to them – and potentially higher prices – because there would be minimal competition. Many individuals and small businesses would find it harder to get loans as banks took little notice of the person asking for the loan, their individual circumstances, or their relationship with the bank.

Small businesses needing loans of less than $100,000 (which represents 50% of all small business loans) and families on the lower rungs of the socio-economic ladder might also find themselves unbanked or underbanked because they are not profitable enough to the institution.

A Great Decision, Not to be Repeated...

As community bankers, we look for people with big ideas so we can help them get their ideas and new businesses off the ground. You identify those people you think are going to run with their ideas and be a success. In 2000, three men came into our office looking for a loan to fund their high-tech start-up – a data security company. They worked in the software security industry and now wanted to follow their dreams. They wanted to create jobs for themselves and be their own bosses.

We saw their passion and their drive. They believed in their product. They had the commitment and the work ethic to see it through. We approved the loan and the business has grown into a spectacular success, creating 400 local, well-paying jobs. The three entrepreneurs have gone global and are leaders in online security. We made the right decision to fund the loan and if we had it to do all over again – we probably wouldn't.

We took a risk back then. The business was based in a rundown industrial park. A rusted garage door opened into cheap rented space. They didn't have a lot of net worth or strength behind them. As a community bank, though, you get to know your customers and you're lending on their character, prior credit performance, the current economic conditions and their potential.

Since the Great Recession, our appetite for risk has diminished. Bank regulators have descended on our bank and pored through our loan portfolio. We have been required to write down millions of dollars in performing loans, based on dropping collateral values and on the outside chance borrowers can't pay. Regulators

(continued on next page)

made us identify risk according to new standards, and now we've exceeded "risk thresholds."

Banks are a lot more gun shy because of the current economy and the regulatory environment. It is more difficult for potential borrowers to qualify for a new loan and credit is not as available as it once was. I would guess a lot of people with great ideas can't get that initial start-up money. This condition has definitely slowed a local and national economic recovery. This is a challenge that the financial industry has found itself in.

Harley Jacobs, President
Capital Community Bank

For all these reasons, the unintended consequences of policies like TARP and Dodd-Frank for community-based financial institutions will make the American Dream harder to achieve. Fewer families will be able to get the mortgages they need to own a home. That means continued sluggishness in the housing market, ongoing reductions in home values, and a reduced ability to use home equity loans to fund auto purchases and educational costs. Small businesses will find it harder and more expensive to access much-needed capital to grow their businesses and hire employees. As a result, job creation will slow and the economy will struggle to achieve meaningful growth. And as job security and financial wealth deteriorate, consumers will become less willing to spend, perpetuating an endless, downward economic cycle.

4: The American Dream Under Pressure

"To stand still is to lose."
Anonymous

The American Dream has always benefited from a nation blessed with vast natural resources, rich reserves of human capital and an enlightened political and economic system that allowed us to become the land of opportunity. This is what attracted generations of immigrants, whose ambition, ideas, and hard work produced more than two and a half centuries of continual improvements in our national strength and our standard of living.

But today, our ideals of prosperity and success are under increasing pressure from the trend toward globalization and emerging (or re-emerging) nations whose industrial and intellectual might is rapidly gaining on – and in some cases overshadowing – that of the U.S. Today, we find ourselves competing not just for markets, but for scarce natural and human resources.

Yet, as troubling as our global challenges may be, they are not the only forces that threaten to undermine the American Dream. Our ideals are equally under pressure from internal forces that include an erosion of values, failed government policies, and a crisis of confidence within our own society.

The importance of maintaining America's position in the global pecking order is more than just a matter of bragging rights and national pride. It goes straight to the heart of preserving the American Dream. If America is no longer able to offer the opportunities and promise of a better life that have defined our society since its inception, if we squander the resources that made us wealthy, if we fail to nourish new ideas and new citizens, we will see many of the traditional sources of America's strength migrate elsewhere.

In fact, we may already be seeing hints of this unwelcome possibility. As members of our own middle-class struggle to keep their jobs, raise their families and make ends meet, people in the industrialized areas of some emerging nations are finding abundant job opportunities, higher incomes (though still nowhere near Western standards), improved access to housing and education, and the ability to enjoy modern conveniences and cultural diversions.

Looking at some of these areas is almost like peering back at America 75 years ago. Of course, it is not quite the same because of the immense income disparities (for instance, in China, just 0.4% of the population possesses approximately 70% of the nation's wealth) and other differences between the select few living in major industrialized zones and the masses living in remote areas. [90] Those in remote areas are often mired in poverty, functionally illiterate, and unable to take advantage of their country's emerging economic bounty.

America has enjoyed a long reign as the world's premier economic superpower, but the world is changing rapidly. Our standing relative to other countries deserves careful attention because it is critical to maintaining our economic viability and our standard of living in the future. To preserve our leadership, we must become more intensely aware of our vulnerabilities and our strengths in a global environment, and operate more effectively within it. We must find ways to participate in the new realities and be willing to make the cultural, political and policy shifts that are necessary. Otherwise, we not only may see the end of the American dream, but also a steady

---

[90] Antoaneta Becker, *Resentment Rises With Widening Wealth Gaps*, Inter Press Service, October 8, 2010.

decline into the shadows of a global marketplace that we helped create. As every investment prospectus notes, "past performance does not guarantee future returns." We cannot allow America to become the land of lost opportunity.

Globalization and the New World Order

Twentieth century advances in communications, information technology, transportation and shipping methods, and international relations (via the International Monetary Fund, the World Bank, the World Trade Organization, the United Nations, the G8 and E7, and so forth) created a complex web of interrelationships among the world's economies. These advances, along with trade agreements and the emergence of worldwide currency exchanges, have turned a patchwork of smaller, provincial economies into a more unified and highly competitive global economy where goods, capital, services and labor flow freely across national borders.

In manufactured goods alone, it is estimated that from 1955 to 2007 global international trade increased more than a hundred-fold, from $95 billion to $12 trillion.[91] The interconnectedness of financial institutions also explains how the U.S. subprime mortgage crisis lit a fuse that ignited bank failures and financial crises around the world, and how concerns about debt levels in Greece and other European countries have created daily gyrations in the U.S. equities markets. The ties among world financial institutions is, in fact, one of our most important learnings about globalization and a factor that must be taken into account in future government and corporate policymaking.

America no longer dominates the global stage as convincingly as we did after World War II and even after the end of the Cold War in

---

[91] Steve Schifferes, "Globalisation Shakes the World," *BBC News*, January 21, 2007.

the 1980s. In fact, the International Monetary Fund estimates that by 2016, the U.S. share of the global economy will fall to 17.7%, in second place behind China, whose share by then is expected to rise to 18%.[92] By the yardstick of growth in industrial production, the current U.S. growth rate of just 5.3% ranks number 77 out of 167 countries, while top-ranked Singapore's growth rate stands at 29.6%; Qatar's at 27.1%, and Taiwan's at 26.4%.[93]

Here are some other disquieting facts about America's position in the new world order:

- The U.S. labor force of 153,900,000 people ranks 4th, behind China (815,300,000 people), India (478,300,000 people) and the E.U. (227,400,000 people).[94]

- The U.S. stock of money, pegged at $1.44 trillion, also ranks 4th behind the E.U. ($5.54 trillion), Japan ($5.42 trillion), and China ($2.44 trillion).[95]

- Wal-Mart, Exxon Mobil, and Chevron were the only U.S.-based companies to reach the top 10 in the latest Fortune ranking of the world's largest global corporations, matched by China's three top 10 companies (Sinopec, China National Petroleum, and State Grid).[96]

- The U.S. broadband penetration rate by population, at 29.8%, ranks 22nd worldwide, well short of leaders Lichtenstein, Luxemburg and Iceland, all of which have penetration rates above 50%.[97]

---

[92] International Monetary Fund, *World Economic Outlook: Tensions from the Two-Speed Recovery*, April 2011.

[93] Central Intelligence Agency, *The CIA World Factbook*, 2010.

[94] Ibid.

[95] Ibid.

[96] "Fortune Global 500," *CNNMoney.com*, July 25, 2011.

[97] Point-Topic, *Global Broadband Statistics*, Q1 2011.

- The soundness of U.S. banks was ranked number 90 out of 142 countries, placing us between banks in Burkina Faso and Ethiopia.[98]

American economic supremacy is under attack. Some of the people I speak with blame the decline in America's stature to a complacency that stems from many years in a leadership position. While there is probably some truth to that perspective, it is not the entire answer. A more complete explanation would have to account for the fact that fast-growing industrial economies (such as China, India, Brazil, Russia and Turkey) have simply become as good as us at what we do.

As we saw in chapter one, the fruits of the American economic system have been long admired and emulated by other nations around the world. Subsequently, many of these countries – whose people long for the same wealth and opportunities that America enjoys – have learned to replicate and even improve upon the model that America originated.

Manufacturing is one example where America has enabled overseas economies to prosper and improve their competitive position. For decades, America was the world's major producer of steel, automobiles, appliances, televisions, electronics and many other items. Today, the bulk of these products is now manufactured offshore and imported into the U.S.

Remember the American television industry? Brands like Zenith, Sylvania, RCA, GE, Magnavox, Westinghouse and Motorola were once famous for producing state-of-the-art, CRT televisions right here in the United States. Today, every one of these brands is either produced overseas or has gone out of business. If you walk into any electronics superstore you will notice that the new leaders are

---

[98] World Economic Forum, *The Global Competitiveness Report 2011-2012*, 2011.

nearly all native Asian brands such as Sony, LG (formerly, "Lucky Goldstar"), Samsung and Panasonic, selling TVs based on far more advanced LED and plasma technologies.

This is not entirely surprising, since America has been undergoing the transition from a labor-based manufacturing economy to a post-industrial knowledge-based economy for many years. Today, the service sector (which includes financial services, healthcare, retailing and business services) has become the largest sector of the U.S. economy, accounting for 76.8% of GDP.[99] As of 2010, the manufacturing sector represented less than 12% of GDP, down from 53% in 1965, despite the fact that overall manufacturing output in the U.S. actually increased during that period. [100]

Of course, America is also a consumption-based economy and since consumers never stopped craving all the "stuff" that our factories used to produce, our demand for imported goods rose as manufacturing moved off-shore. This helps to explain why overseas manufacturing has grown significantly over the past 40-plus years and why the U.S. trade deficit (the difference between the goods we produce and the goods we buy from abroad) stood somewhere around $500 billion dollars in 2011.[101]

In addition to aiding foreign businesses through our appetite for their goods, America also educated large numbers of foreign businessmen, scientists, engineers and entrepreneurs at our top colleges and universities. This is a trend that continues today, as foreign enrollment at U.S. schools reached an all-time high of nearly 724,000 in 2010/11.[102]

[99] Central Intelligence Agency, *The CIA World Factbook*, 2010.
[100] U.S. Bureau of Economic Analysis.
[101] U.S. Census Bureau, Jan-Sept 2011 Seasonally Adjusted U.S. Trade in Goods with World.
[102] Institute of International Education, *2011 Open Doors Report on International Educational Exchange* (Leetsdale, PA: IIEBooks, November 15, 2011).

Not surprisingly, many of these skilled professionals are starting to pursue opportunities back in their native lands, bringing with them valuable knowledge and training that will make their countries more powerful competitors against the U.S.

The American consumers' desire for affordable goods combined with our country's willingness to share its know-how has catalyzed a major shift in manufacturing to lower-cost regions of the world, particularly for goods and services that are now commoditized. As we continue to purchase these goods and services, we will become increasingly dependent on sources outside the U.S. to supply them and increasingly leave behind a manufacturing capability that used to make us unique.

Offsetting this trend, of course, is the demand in emerging countries for important products and services that America still does produce, many of which are based on our knowledge economy. This includes financial, management and executive expertise; software and entertainment products; as well as more traditional agricultural products, advanced machinery, aircraft, automobiles, weapons, medical devices and pharmaceuticals.

Many American companies (think GE, Boeing, Lockheed Martin, Microsoft, Altria, Dow Chemical, Exxon Mobil, Apple, IBM, Intel, Ford, GM, Colgate-Palmolive, Merck, Johnson & Johnson, Amazon, Levi's, Coca-Cola, McDonalds, Starbucks and Disney, to name a few) have benefitted greatly from international expansion. In fact, it has been estimated that over 45% of the profits for firms in the S&P 500 stock index now come from overseas.[103]

Still, inconsistencies in labor policy, legal systems, human rights and economic rights around the world have raised clear warning signs about growing trade inequities, despite the efforts of the World Trade

---

[103] Howard Silverblatt, *S&P 500: 2010 Global Sales*, July 19, 2011.

Organization to maintain a level playing field. For example, lax or non-existent trademark and copyright protection in other countries has fostered widespread counterfeiting of American products – a large proportion of which are digital products such as movies, recordings and software. According to the most recent estimate by the Organisation for Economic Co-operation and Development (OECD), the value of counterfeited and pirated goods sold outside the country in which they are produced amounts to at least $250 billion each year. And the large number of counterfeit goods sold within the countries where they are produced adds another $150 to $200 billion to this total.[104]

In order for America to compete in the global economy, we need to eliminate inequities and unfair trade practices as much as possible. Our imports of foreign manufacturing-based goods and services must be offset by exports of our own knowledge-based goods and services, for which we must receive fair value. We also need fair access to the markets of countries that are our trading partners so that, for instance, Google can operate without restrictions on its content in China, and Microsoft can compete in markets where counterfeiting makes illegal versions of Office available for as little as $5.

We should also be aware that as America struggles to reestablish its economic prominence in world markets, our competitors are rapidly working their way up the economic value chain and transitioning from being low-cost producers to new-product innovators. American companies that used to count on retaining domestic jobs in high-value, knowledge-based endeavors while exporting lower-value tasks overseas can no longer rely on this strategy. With the rapid spread of advanced computer, communications and networking technologies, we are now seeing a growing number of high-value, white-collar

---

[104] Organisation for Economic Co-operation and Development, *Magnitude of Counterfeiting and Piracy of Tangible Products: An Update*, November 18, 2009.

positions in accounting, software development, engineering, and other areas move overseas, just as manufacturing jobs did before them.

The long-term impact of rising economic powerhouses like China, India and Russia remains to be seen, but we have already witnessed their dramatic effect on prices, jobs, demand for energy and natural resources, and the environment, among other things. What is abundantly clear is that America must work even harder in the future to remain competitive in global markets and to preserve the American Dream.

Effects of Economic Evolution

Looking ahead, I expect today's emerging industrial nations to evolve along a path similar to the one America followed in its own evolution from an industrial-based to a knowledge-based economy. We can already see this happening in China, as it moves from the role of being a low-cost producer toward the role of innovator and original product designer.

What typically happens when a group of people satisfies its most basic needs is that their focus then shifts toward the satisfaction of higher-level needs, as the psychologist Abraham Maslow pointed out in his studies of human motivation. Thus, as China, India, Russia, Brazil and other nations have developed stronger manufacturing economies, they have seen a concomitant rise in wages, consumer demand, housing and education, and the emergence of a growing middle class. In fact, the World Bank estimates that the global middle class is likely to grow from 430 million in 2000 to 1.15 billion in 2030, with China and India accounting for two-thirds of the global expansion.[105]

---

[105] The World Bank, *Global Economic Prospects 2007: Managing the Next Wave of Globalization* (Washington, DC: World Bank, 2007).

As this trend continues, I expect two things to happen. First, today's powerful industrial economies will become equally powerful knowledge economies that will eventually compete with America in new areas, such as information technology, pharmaceuticals, alternative energy, genetic engineering, and finance, to name just a few.

This has already happened in places like Bangalore, India, where Indian customer support personnel are fielding calls for Dell computer owners in the U.S.; reservation agents are booking flights for Delta airlines customers; software engineers are developing new applications for Oracle and other tech companies; and accountants are preparing tax returns for American clients of Ernst & Young.

Second, I expect that the growing middle classes in emerging countries will exert the same wage, price, resource and labor challenges that America faces today. Their workers will no longer want to work in factories, but instead will seek higher-paying, white collar jobs. Demand for housing and affordable consumer goods will drive domestic prices higher, which in turn will give rise to imports from a new generation of emerging manufacturing economies...where the cycle will begin again.

As other cultures and economies evolve and become more like our own, the challenge for America is to lead the way in creating a level playing field among our competitors and committing ourselves to outperform. It is in every nation's long-term interest to create a vibrant global economy where open markets thrive and competition is driven by innovation and superiority. But even as we pursue this goal, America needs to address the state of our competitive capabilities if we expect to maintain a seat at the head of the table.

Education: Second to None?

One of the most important keys to maintaining America's competitive position in the global marketplace is ensuring an educational system that prepares our workforce to face tomorrow's challenges. America currently has the fifth highest overall educational expenditures as a percentage of GDP in the world, as well as the second highest expenditures per pupil.[106] But in comparison with other educational systems around the globe, our outsized expenditures have delivered only an average educational result.

For instance, in 2009, the Paris-based OECD conducted a study comparing educational systems in 74 countries, administering standardized tests to over a half million 15-year-olds to determine their relative proficiency in math, literacy and science. When the results were in, the top five spots went to Shanghai-China, Hong Kong-China, Finland, Singapore, and Japan, respectively. The U.S. ranked 26th overall (scoring 17st in reading, 31st in math, and 23rd in science).[107]

This is not necessarily indicative of a decline in the quality of American compulsory education. According to a recent Brookings Institution report, U.S. scores have actually improved since the 1960s, when the first international math tests were administered. Back then, the U.S. ranked next to last, at number 11 out of 12 countries.[108] The key point is that other nations have adopted and improved upon the American educational model – just as they did with the American economic model – and are now outperforming us on it.

---

[106] Organisation for Economic Co-operation and Development, *Education at a Glance 2011: Highlights*, 2011.

[107] Organisation for Economic Co-operation and Development, *PISA 2009 Results: Executive Summary*, 2010.

[108] Tom Loveless, *2010 Brown Center Report on American Education* (Washington, DC: Brookings Institution, 2010).

What makes education rates so important is that they bear a direct relationship to economic performance. Good education means access to good jobs and higher earnings, and a lifetime of higher earnings equals a larger and more stable economy. There is clearly an opportunity for America to reap the benefits of improved education rates. According to a 2009 McKinsey report: "If the United States had in recent years closed the gap between its educational achievement levels and those of better-performing nations such as Finland and Korea, GDP in 2008 could have been $1.3 trillion to $2.3 trillion higher. This represents 9 to 16% of GDP."[109]

Comparing U.S. college graduation rates to the rates in other countries shows another area where global competitors have taken an American idea and run with it. Less than a generation ago, the U.S. led the world in the percentage of 25- to 34-year-olds graduating with an associate's degree or higher. Today, our graduation rate stands at 40.4%, or 12th place globally. The top five spots are now held by Canada, Korea, the Russian Federation, Japan and New Zealand.[110] The College Board, reflecting on these statistics, recently issued a blunt assessment: "The percentage of American adults with postsecondary credentials is not keeping pace with other industrialized nations."[111]

Moreover, other nations' commitment to quality education seems to reflect a basic cultural change, and not simply the outcome of local school investments or resources. Evidence of this comes from the relatively high performance of foreign students attending U.S. schools. Thomas Friedman alluded to this fact in a recent editorial in the *New York Times*:

---

[109] McKinsey & Company, *The Economic Impact of the Achievement Gap in America's Schools*, April 2009: 5.

[110] John Michael Lee, Jr. and Anita Rawls, *The College Completion Agenda: 2010 Progress Report*, The College Board, 2010.

[111] The College Board, November 17, 2011, http://completionagenda. collegeboard.org/.

Last week, the 32 winners of Rhodes Scholarships for 2011 were announced — America's top college grads. Here are half the names on that list: Mark Jia, Aakash Shah, Zujaja Tauqeer, Tracy Yang, William Zeng, Daniel Lage, Ye Jin Kang, Baltazar Zavala, Esther Uduehi, Prerna Nadathur, Priya Sury, Anna Alekeyeva, Fatima Sabar, Renugan Raidoo, Jennifer Lai, Varun Sivaram. Do you see a pattern? [112]

Given the direct relationship between educational performance and per capita income, it is essential for America to renew its commitment to quality education. We need to continue improving our basic curriculums, boosting our graduation rates, and making sure that the money we devote to education delivers measurable academic results. If we fail to keep pace with or fall further behind the other nations that have adopted our commitment to education, we will find ourselves at a significant competitive disadvantage that places our future prosperity in jeopardy.

The Threat to Innovation

As global competition heats up and our competitors move further up the value-chain, innovation also plays a vital role in maintaining America's competitive position. Because innovation creates jobs and enlarges the economy, scientific knowledge, ideas and technical skills have literally become our most valuable natural resources. They are the raw materials needed to energize the breakthroughs that will define 21st century global commerce.

America has a proud history of innovation. From the cotton gin to the light bulb, from the telephone to the Model T Ford, from the airplane to the space shuttle, from the PC to social networking sites, we have consistently combined basic research with scientific, engineering and

---

[112] Thomas L. Friedman, "U.S.G. and P.T.A.," *New York Times*, November 23, 2010.

marketing know-how to create economically viable new products. America still accounts for 34% of the world's spending on R&D and is second only to Japan in the total number of patent families issued (patent applications related to the same subject matter that are applied for in multiple countries).[113]

But here again, other countries are catching up and moving forward. As the chart below shows, forecasted R&D spending in the U.S., Europe and Japan actually declined between 2010 and 2012, while China and India increased their investments in R&D.

Figure 22 - Global R&D Spending in Top Five Regions, 2010 & 2012

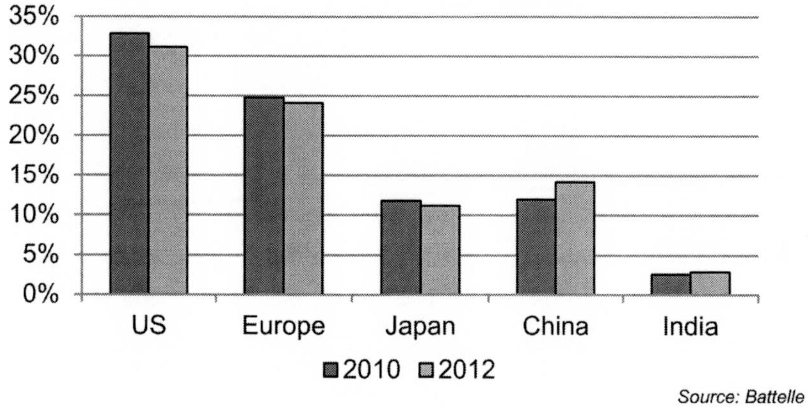

Source: Battelle

Similarly, the number of U.S patent family applications remained nearly constant between 2000 and 2007, while Chinese patent applications increased more than five-fold.[114]

---

[113] Batelle, *2011 Global R&D Funding Forecast*, R&D Magazine, December 2010.

[114] World Intellectual Property Organization, *World Intellectual Property Indicators 2010*, September 2010.

Figure 23 - Patent Families by Country of Origin (Top Five Countries), 2000-2007

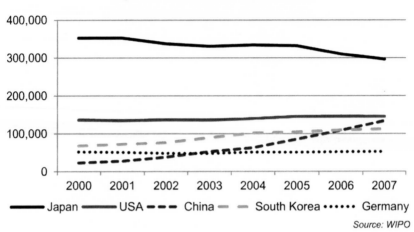

Source: WIPO

Here's another eye-opening metric: in 2008, America led the World Economic Forum's Global Competitiveness Index, a widely followed ranking of countries' overall competitive environment based on multiple factors including the strength of a country's institutions, infrastructure, laws, market dynamics, and so on. By 2011, the U.S. had slipped to fifth place – behind Switzerland, Singapore, Sweden and Finland. In its analysis of the rankings, the Forum cited high levels of U.S. debt, excessive government regulation, and government waste of resources as a few of the reasons for the U.S. decline.[115]

America's lead in innovation is at risk for several reasons. These include an educational system that doesn't adequately emphasize basic science and math skills, disproportionate investments in engineering and research centers being made by our global neighbors, and flawed immigration policies that result in a large number of foreign-born PhDs no longer seeking their fortunes in the U.S.

---

[115] World Economic Forum, *The Global Competitiveness Report 2011-2012,* 2011.

We have already discussed the relatively low science and math scores that U.S. students received in the international exams conducted by the OECD. Regarding research centers, we have seen well-financed new facilities being constructed by our competitors around the globe for several years now. For example, the Russian government is building a "scientific city" near Moscow that is modeled on the U.S.'s own Silicon Valley and intended to be an innovation incubator for promising new technologies. Meanwhile, the Chinese government recently announced a plan to more than double the number of its country's university-based science parks, from 86 in 2011 to 200 by 2015.[116]

Israel's Ministry of Industry Trade & Labor, which began developing business incubators in the 1990s, now operates 27 of these centers around the country.[117] The centers are devoted largely to basic scientific R&D and early-stage technology development, and much of the operating costs for the centers is paid for by royalties from the companies that were hatched within.

In addition to government- and university-sponsored research facilities, corporate research centers are also budding overseas. As American multinational companies move their manufacturing operations to other countries, the research centers that fuel them (and that once grew up around America's manufacturing hubs) are moving, as well.

The Reverse Brain Drain

I mentioned in chapter one how the talent and drive of skilled immigrants pursuing their dreams has been one of America's greatest

---

[116] Bi Mingxin, ed., "China to Cultivate 3,000 University-Based Technological Start-Ups in Five Years," *Xinhua News Agency*, August 2011.

[117] Israel Business Connection, "Technological Incubators," November 2011, http://www.israelbusiness.org.il.

competitive advantages, and it is an advantage that continues today. In fact, a nationwide study on entrepreneurs showed that fully 25.3% of the technology and engineering companies that started in the U.S. between 1995 and 2005 had at least one foreign-born founder. [118]

But today, there is an emerging class of foreign-born technical professionals with entrepreneurial ambitions who are discovering that Silicon Valley is not the only place to find abundant venture capital, sophisticated computing and network infrastructure, a deep technical talent pool, and the right creative mojo. They are finding similar characteristics back home in Bangalore, Singapore, Beijing, Moscow and other international technology hubs. They are also finding rewarding economic opportunities, as America struggles to lift itself from the financial crisis and a prolonged recession.

While the lure of family and a familiar culture are certainly part of the reason why many of these professionals return to their native lands, U.S. immigration policy is also partly at fault. America, a nation of immigrants, has made it increasingly difficult for foreign-born entrepreneurs to get permanent visas that would allow them to fully develop their talents and start businesses in the U.S. Meanwhile, the temporary H-1B visas we provide to skilled professionals do not encourage business formation, because they tie workers to a single employer. This makes returning to their own country the only option for striking out on their own in business.

Is this the beginning of a new "brain drain" that will end America's long history of attracting and nurturing the world's most promising entrepreneurs? Only time will tell.

For the moment, America still offers significant cultural and other advantages to aspiring technology and engineering professionals.

---

[118] Vivek Wadhwa, "Open Doors Wider for Skilled Immigrants," *Bloomberg Businessweek*, January 2007.

Despite reduced investments in recent years, our university- and government-based research organizations remain the largest and most sophisticated in the world. We offer the world's strongest protections for intellectual property rights. We have the largest and most accessible pools of private venture capital. And we have a culture that rewards free thinking like no other; we are always open to new ideas, and we regard failure not as an act of shame, but as the natural consequence of taking big risks. These are all qualities that we need to preserve to keep America on innovation's cutting edge and provide the most attractive opportunities for tomorrow's generation of engineers and technologists.

Congratulations! You failed.

Many an American entrepreneur's path to success has been paved with failure. For example, automaker Henry Ford founded two car companies that went bankrupt before he launched today's Ford Motor Company. Walt Disney's first animation studio was also a bust. Fred Smith, the founder of FedEx, got a near-failing grade when he presented the idea for an overnight package delivery service to his business management class at Yale. Bill Gates and Paul Allen ran a now-defunct company to measure roadway traffic before founding Microsoft. Mark Cuban failed in multiple business enterprises (including bartending, disco dance instruction, and software retailing) before becoming a successful serial entrepreneur. Today, he is the Chairman of HDNet, owner of the Dallas Mavericks, the Landmark Theatre chain, Magnolia Pictures, the Bailoutsleuth.com Web site, and founder of many other ventures. What these individuals and many others like them all have in common is the desire to change the world, an appetite for risk, and the ability to gain insight from previous mistakes... hallmarks of America's unique culture of innovation.

Louis Hernandez, Jr.

Changing Attitudes and Misguided Policies

As if the external pressures confronting America aren't daunting enough, internal pressures – including the erosion of fundamental values and increased government involvement in our daily economic lives – are adding to the challenges of maintaining American competitiveness in the global marketplace.

Earlier, I said that American complacency did not, of itself, sufficiently explain America's declining competitive position. But complacency does account for some of the problem, along with a succession of government policies that consistently fall short of their intended goals.

When I survey America today and reflect back on the fundamental principles of the American Dream – providing the freedom and opportunity for each person to fulfill their innate potential and pursue a better position in life – I can't help but think that as a society we have veered from the original intent of this remarkable dream. Our parents and grandparents probably understood its true meaning more profoundly. They understood that the dream promised only an opportunity, not a right. They understood that taking advantage of this opportunity would require patience, sacrifice, personal responsibility, hard work and financial prudence on their part. They understood that the dream was intended to provide a leg up, not a handout.

I believe that many Americans have lost sight of the personal attributes required to achieve the dream and have succumbed to the belief that somehow, by simply waking up in America, good fortune is our right. We have forgotten that all of America's successes came through great sacrifice – both in terms of personal hardship and in hard-fought wars to preserve democracy. If we are unwilling to work as hard or perform the jobs that our immigrant forebears were eager to do, perhaps it is because we fail to appreciate how much better life is in America than elsewhere in the world. Perhaps we have forgotten

126

what it means to sacrifice and save to improve our standard of living, because we have the ability to gain immediate gratification through borrowing and can live well beyond our means. Some of us have even stopped taking personal responsibility for the quality of our lives within our communities, passing these concerns on to community organizations and our elected officials. It saddens me to think that a single generation could squander what so many prior generations worked extremely hard to achieve.

This is not intended as a condemnation of all Americans; I know there are many hard-working, committed people with strong values in this country. I spend much of my life traveling and I meet these people every day, along with equally committed, hard-working people in the other countries I visit. But I sense a general trend that Americans are moving away from our traditional sources of strength and the deeper meanings of the American Dream, just as people in other countries are embracing them more fully.

By the same token, I believe the American government has sometimes hopelessly misunderstood and overstepped its role as a facilitator of the American Dream. Instead of simply providing the freedom to pursue a better position in life, it promoted policies aimed at making the dream almost too easy to achieve while calibrating its benchmarks toward quantity instead of quality.

In housing, it was government guarantees and targeted subprime mortgage lending policies that allowed many people to get into homes who truly couldn't afford them. Now, many of these same people are homeless and our banking system is buried under an avalanche of bad loans, soured derivatives and foreclosed properties.

America's monetary policy, which kept interest rates low and made credit easily available to consumers, enabled many people to enjoy a standard of living that was well beyond their means, but at the cost of going deeply into debt. Today, large numbers of these people are unemployed and struggling to repay existing loans, while creditworthy borrowers are finding it nearly impossible to get new loans. Taxpayers who lived within their means are the real losers here; their homes are underwater, they have received no relief on their debt, and their taxes are supporting the bailout of others who were less financially prudent.

Our educational policies, too, have been aimed at increasing public school graduation rates and getting students into college. The result has been a generation of graduates who emerge from college with fewer skills than our global competitors, overwhelming student loan obligations, and diminished job prospects due to high unemployment. Meanwhile, we continually churn out more liberal arts and business graduates than American businesses can absorb, while failing to produce enough graduates with the scientific and technical skills needed to compete in the future.

Figure 24 - Bachelor's Degrees by Selected Fields of Study, 1988-2009

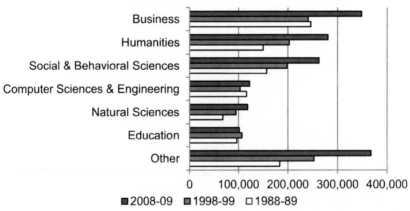

Source: U.S. Dept. of Education

American policies have also made it more challenging than ever to start and run a small business. Excessive regulations consume valuable business resources and increase costs, making American products and services more expensive. At the same time, high corporate taxes and fees drain profits, while toughened lending standards and capital constraints make it hard for community-based financial institutions to give small businesses the credit they need to grow and hire employees.

Crisis of Confidence

Today I see a growing perception that America's best days may soon be behind us. A sense that the little guy doesn't stand a chance against large, powerful interests, and that the American Dream is increasingly out of reach. We are reeling from the recessionary fallout of the housing bust and the financial crisis, and living in a time when people worry about losing their jobs (if they haven't already lost them). Retirement savings have been decimated, wages have remained essentially flat for nearly a decade, consumer spending has pulled back, businesses are afraid to invest because they are uncertain about the future, and banks are hesitant to lend.

There is a crisis in confidence in America. People have started to lose faith in their institutions and their futures. Study after study shows that we have not solved the problem of rebuilding this confidence, rebuilding the economy, or rebuilding the American Dream. And the loss of confidence has had a stagnating effect on our economy.

In a recent *Newsweek* poll, 68% of respondents said they were dissatisfied with the way things are going in the United States. Respondents overwhelmingly blamed the U.S. Congress as a whole (59%) for their dissatisfaction and said the top reasons they were dissatisfied were economic conditions in general (75%), government spending and the federal deficit (68%), and the way the government and the political system are working (65%). What worried respondents most were economic issues, which included having enough savings for retirement (66%), maintaining their current standard of living

(63%), and being able to pay medical or health care costs (62%). Looking forward, 76% said they were somewhat worried or very worried about the future. [119]

Raddon Financial Group noticed a similar lack of confidence in the economy among consumers. In their most recent consumer survey, Raddon found that 69% of U.S. households saw no evidence that the recession was over, despite seven consecutive quarters of GDP growth. And looking ahead, most consumers expected the economy to remain about the same for the next six months, while 23% expected it to be worse. [120]

The consumer outlook for the overall economy improved from where it was during the depths of the recession in the fall of 2008, but Raddon's research showed that recent gains were only marginally better than six months earlier…or even 12 months earlier. Overall, their data revealed four straight years where consumers were generally more likely to believe things would get worse rather than better.[121]

Figure 25 - Consumer Economic Expectations, 2007-2011

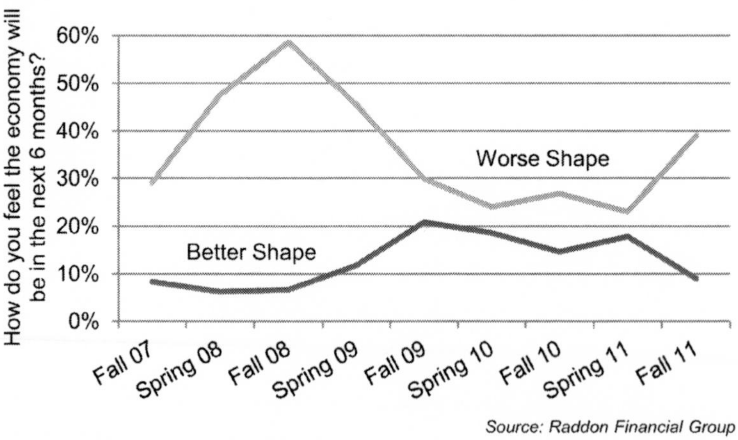

Source: Raddon Financial Group

---

[119] "Psychology of Voter Anger," *Newsweek*, October 10, 2010.
[120] Raddon Financial Group, *Fall 2011 National Consumer Survey*, October 2011.
[121] Ibid.

Raddon also reported that consumers anticipated little improvement in their personal financial situation for the next six months. Of those surveyed, most (55%) expected their financial situation to remain about the same, while 19% expected it to be worse.[122]

Figure 26 - Consumer Expectations for Personal Financial Situation, 2011

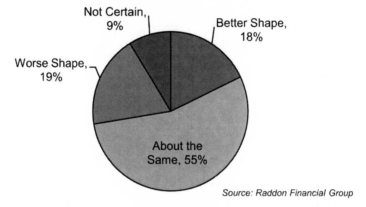

Source: Raddon Financial Group

One consequence of reduced consumer confidence has been the emergence of a new frugality that's being driven by the recession, depressed home values and an uncertain financial outlook. As Raddon's research confirms, a little over half of consumers stated that they are spending less today than in the previous year, 38% were spending about the same, and only 8% claimed to be spending more.[123]

Like consumers, small businesses also lack confidence in the future and see little prospect for improved economic conditions on the horizon. The National Federation of Independent Business (NFIB) Small Business Optimism Index, which consolidates 10 forward-looking components of small business operations, shows small business optimism has been stuck below the baseline 100 level since 2007.[124]

---

[122] Ibid.

[123] Ibid.

[124] William C. Dunkelberg and Holly Wade, *NFIB Small Business Economic Trends*, November 2011.

Figure 27 - Small Business Optimism, 2004-2011

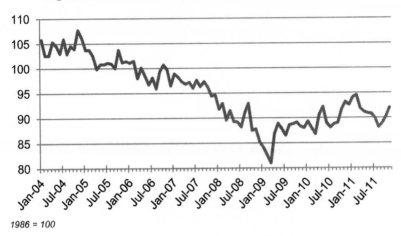

1986 = 100

Source: National Federation for Independent Business

One especially interesting aspect of this index is that it shows small business optimism dipping below the baseline as early as 1Q 2006, indicating that small businesses may have been among the first to feel the tremors of the coming recession.[125]

Adding further support to the bleak business confidence outlook, Raddon Financial Group's Fall 2011 Small Business survey found that when businesses were asked to forecast 2011 sales in comparison to 2010, the majority were predicting that 2011 sales would be as bad or worse than in 2010, a year in which sales were already severely depressed.[126]

---

[125] Ibid.

[126] Raddon Financial Group, *Fall 2011 National Small Business Survey*, October 2011.

Figure 28 - Small Business Expectations for Sales Growth, 2011

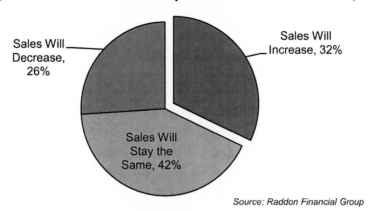

Source: Raddon Financial Group

As I noted before, small businesses are the primary drivers of new employment in the U.S. Declining confidence combined with restrictive government policies and a lack of credit, especially from larger banks, only serve to magnify the challenges that America faces in the years ahead.

So that is the core of our problem today. America suffers from declining power amidst growing global competition, education rates that are not up to the level of our peers, competitive and policy impediments that are choking off innovation, a population that has grown out of touch with the core values of the American Dream, a government whose policies occasionally do as much harm as good, and a loss of confidence in the economy and the future that has taken hold of consumers and businesses alike.

In a 2010 poll by Zogby International, only 57% of respondents said they thought it was possible for themselves and their families to achieve the American Dream. This is a sizable drop from the 76% who thought that achieving the dream was possible just nine years earlier, in 2001. [127] This is not a course we want to be on. It's time for a moment of clarity, to re-examine who we are and why we're here, to reevaluate our

---

[127] Zogby International, *Zogby Interactive: Belief in Attaining American Dream Now 57%*, March 18, 2010.

policies and beliefs, to abandon practices that undermine a sustainable American Dream, and to reposition ourselves to win.

Dusting Off and Continuing the Dream...

Wabash is the county seat of a small rural community in northern Indiana. The city's website features images of a fire truck, an old mill and a sunset – emblems of life here. We're a community of people that encourage each other and when one of us falls, someone's there to pick them up. Very often, our credit union is the one to dust someone off and give them a second chance.

For example, we'd been buying our office supplies from a well-established, local Mom-and-Pop store for many years, until the recession landed them in bankruptcy. They lost their business and their home, but not their ambition.

One day, the couple came to us for a loan to start over again, with a new office supply business. We could have found reasons to say 'No,' but that's not our philosophy. Instead, we looked for ways to make a loan to put the couple back into business, and we did – but it was all because of their character and not their collateral.

We stepped out on a limb for this couple when others wouldn't, and now we've seen them flourish. It is very satisfying to help borrowers fulfill their aspirations. We're trying to make this community a better place to live, work and raise a family. It's all about serving your neighbors and helping them realize their dreams.

The American Dream can mean falling, failing and starting over again – many times. It's important to stick with people in good times and bad.

Bruce Ingraham, President
Beacon Credit Union

5: Reviving the American Dream

"Putting people first has always been America's secret weapon. It's the way we've kept the spirit of our revolutions alive—a spirit that drives us to dream and dare, and take great risks for a greater good." [128]
Ronald Reagan

Throughout this book I have pointed out how many of our global competitors' achievements are inspired by and modeled upon the success of the American dream. Regardless of how America rates against these competitors on certain contemporary metrics, there is no doubt that there is more freedom and democracy in the world today than there has ever been before. There are more opportunities for improving one's standard of living, with middle classes emerging in countries that once knew only widespread poverty and highly concentrated wealth. There is better education, and greater cooperation among nations than at any other time in the world's history.

These are achievements that we can all be proud of because they demonstrate the power of the American Dream and not, as some would have it, a decline in America's influence. There should be no mistake: America is still the world's greatest economic and military superpower, the wealthiest nation, the most prolific center of innovation, and the most open society. What the latest metrics indicate, however, is that America must re-embrace and renew our commitment to the American Dream – as other nations have – to

---

[128] Ronald Reagan, Radio Message on the Observance of Independence Day, July 3, 1981.

maintain the prosperity and the standard of excellence that have been our hallmarks for so long.

As part of re-embracing the American Dream, we must always remember that the underlying principles of this dream are based on individual effort and personal responsibility. No one ever promised that we could enjoy the wealth and prosperity that America offered without personally taking the steps needed to achieve it.

I believe the time has come for each of us individually – and the American public collectively – to accept personal responsibility for our American Dream again. It is time to rethink our beliefs and expectations, and to ask our government to reexamine the direction and implications of its policies. It is time to restore American competitiveness by recommitting ourselves to leadership in education, entrepreneurship and innovation while rebuilding consumer and small business confidence. It is time to return health and fairness to our financial system while creating an environment that allows smaller financial institutions to continue fulfilling their role as the cornerstone of America's communities.

I know that we can succeed in this task because America has always had the quality of adaptability. Just look at how we responded to the attack on Pearl Harbor in 1941, the terrorist assault of September 11, 2001, and the financial crisis of 2008. Our adaptability is a great cultural advantage that America has over other countries, and it is a quality that has become essential in today's rapidly changing world.

Restoring Competitiveness

In almost every way, the economies of the world have become larger, more interconnected and interdependent. Overall output and GDP are increasing worldwide. Emerging industrial nations are quickly rising to become rich, developed economies. Technology is bringing together market players in ways that were barely imaginable 50 years ago. Education levels and infrastructure increasingly are making it possible for goods and services to be produced anywhere around the globe.

Today, more than 46% of the profits for companies in the S&P 500 come from outside the U.S.[129] Successful companies – like IBM, Coca-Cola, Google, Microsoft, Apple, and Caterpillar – have learned to navigate and thrive on the global playing field by adopting global best practices, measuring themselves against global standards, creating distributed workforces around the world, and collaborating effectively with suppliers and partners in diverse local geographies.

America as a nation must learn to do the same. As the competitive landscape extends its borders and grows more challenging, it is imperative to raise our game and begin seriously addressing macro issues in areas that include education, innovation and entrepreneurship to position ourselves to win.

Maintaining Leadership in Science and Technology

The American higher education system is generally regarded as the finest in the world. According to *U.S. News & World Report*, we are home to six of the top ten universities worldwide.[130] But dig a little deeper and a different picture emerges of a higher education system that is falling behind competitors in much of Western Europe and advanced Asian nations – such as China, Japan and South Korea – at the topmost levels in science, technology, engineering and math (also known as STEM) disciplines.

---

[129] Howard Silverblatt, *S&P 500: 2010 Global Sales*, July 19, 2011.
[130] U.S. News & World Report, *World's Best Universities: Top 400*, 2011, http://www.usnews.com/education/worlds-best-universities-rankings/top-400-universities-in-the-world.

This is an area of great personal concern to me, both as a technology professional and as the former Vice-Chair of the Governor's Council on Economic Competitiveness and Technology in my home state of Connecticut. I have spent a great deal of time researching and working to promote STEM fields, and it troubles me when I see that there are more undergraduates majoring in the visual and performing arts than in engineering and related technologies in this country.[131]

Graduate and postgraduate education in the STEM fields is crucial because these fields are the foundation of American innovation and entrepreneurism in the 21st century. While other fields of study, such as the visual and performing arts, are certainly important in our society, they need to be balanced with STEM degrees, which are the foundation of a knowledge-based economy and will be the primary drivers of future job opportunities. As noted in a recent publication by United States National Academies:

> *Because other nations have, and probably will continue to have the competitive advantage of low-wage structure, the United States must compete by optimizing its knowledge-based resources, particularly in science and technology, and by sustaining the most fertile environment for new and revitalized industries and the well-paying jobs they bring.*[132]

The variety of STEM fields reads like a Who's Who of emerging technologies. In addition to basic math, physics and chemistry, it includes disciplines such as acoustical engineering, aerospace engineering, astrophysics, atmospheric sciences, biochemistry, bioinformatics, biomechanics, chemical engineering, chemistry, civil

---

[131] Susan Aud et al., *The Condition of Education 2011* (Washington, DC: U.S. Dept. of Education, May 2011).

[132] National Academy of Sciences, National Academy of Engineering, and Institute of Medicine, *Rising Above the Gathering Storm: Energizing and Employing America for a Brighter Future* (Washington, DC: The National Academies Press, 2007).

engineering, computer engineering, computer science, cyberinfra-structure, electrical engineering, geographic information systems, geoscience, materials science, mathematical biology, mechanical engineering, nanotechnology, neurobiology, nuclear physics, robotics, and many others.

While the absolute number of science- and engineering-related (S&E) degrees awarded by U.S. institutions has generally risen year-over-year since the mid-1980s, there are signs that more needs to be done to remain competitive on a global scale. According to recent statistics from the National Science Board: [133]

- In the United States, S&E degrees are about one-third of bachelor's degrees. By comparison, S&E-related degrees represented more than half of the first degrees awarded in Japan (63%), China (53%), and Singapore (51%) in 2006.

- Foreign students received 24% of the master's degrees and 33% of the doctoral degrees awarded by U.S. institutions in S&E in 2007.

- The number of S&E-related first university degrees awarded in China, Poland, and Taiwan more than doubled between 1998 and 2006.

---

[133] National Science Board, *Science and Engineering Indicators: 2010* (Arlington, VA: National Science Foundation, January 2010).

Figure 29 - First University Degrees in Natural Sciences and Engineering (selected countries), 1998-2006

(Thousands)

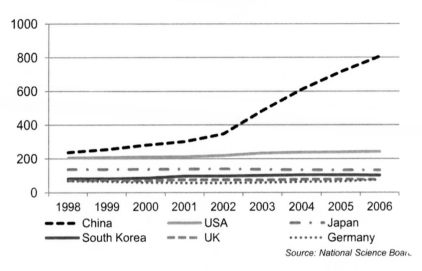

Source: National Science Board

One reason why the U.S. is becoming less competitive at the highest levels of STEM education is because we are not staying competitive in basic science and math at the secondary school level. The World Economic Forum recently ranked the U.S. 51st in overall quality of our secondary math and science education.[134] And, as I pointed out in chapter 4, the U.S. scored 31st in math and 23rd in science on the most recent international secondary education rankings by the OECD.

What I didn't discuss was that a major reason for our poor showing has been the growing shortage of qualified secondary school teachers in math and science. Again, according to the National Science Board:

Nationally between 17 percent and 28 percent of public high school science teachers, depending on field, and 20 percent of mathematics teachers lacked full certification in their teaching field in 2002; the problem was proportionally higher for middle grades. Although most mathematics and science

---

[134] World Economic Forum, *The Global Competitiveness Report 2011-2012*, 2011.

teachers hold a bachelor's degree, many are teaching sub-jects for which they have had little or no training. [135]

Experts cite two major reasons for the lack of qualified teachers in math and science: the attrition of qualified teachers from the teaching profession and the more attractive career alternatives for science and math graduates who might otherwise consider teaching. Regardless of the reason, none of this bodes well for the future of American innovation and entrepreneurism.

Intensive Care for the American Dream...

I believe medical miracles can happen in the most unlikely places – even the local branch of a credit union. Our mission at the National Institutes of Health Federal Credit Union (NIHFCU) is more like our heartbeat: to serve recent college and university graduates entering the biomedical and healthcare professions in Maryland, Virginia, Washington DC and West Virginia.

These men and women are among the best and brightest in America, conducting biomedical research and making breakthroughs that prevent illness and save lives. But when they graduate, they're saddled with debt – student loans and credit card bills that can approach $250,000. Students who backburner their mounting debt when they're in school see a tsunami of loan payments come due when they graduate.

Biomedical researchers make very little money. They're like the early inventors, working in humble laboratories and austere incubators with virtually no funding. Their debt to income ratio

(continued on next page)

---

[135] National Science Board, *A Companion to Science and Engineering Indicators: 2006* (Arlington, VA: National Science Foundation, January 2006).

is so strained, they need financial assistance that major financial institutions typically aren't willing to provide. This is where our intensive care helps restore the financial health of these medical professionals.

We study their financial profiles, meet at their homes and work with them individually to restructure debt and develop customized loan solutions. We help them create plans that lead to positive credit scores, get them into their first homes and prudently manage school debt. We drill down to the person, examining what they have and need with more flexibility and personal attention than larger banks can offer with their high throughput operations and standardized programs.

Member service isn't a seven-minute, click-through transaction. It's consulting with people and listening to their goals and challenges. Many of our members live humbly and work hard because they believe in their solutions – and because we believe in them, we find ways to relieve their financial stress.

Juli Anne Callis, President and CEO
National Institutes of Health Federal Credit Union

Even as Federal budgets remain under tremendous pressure, it is essential to choose program funding wisely and with an eye toward America's future. From my perspective, there is no wiser investment we can make than our investment in science and technology education, which is so intimately linked with our nation's current and future economic needs. The explanation is simple: science and technology education drives innovation; innovation drives entrepreneurship; entrepreneurship drives employment and wealth; and employment and wealth drive the prosperity that is the basis of the American Dream.

Our investment in education should include direct Federal funding for academic R&D expenditures, which has been declining since 2004; improving secondary teacher education in science and math disciplines; improving secondary teacher salaries to recruit more qualified prospects into the field; and aligning our academic expectations to international standards.[136]

We have already seen promise in programs that expose younger kids to the excitement of science and technology – and lay the foundation for their future education – in magnet schools where such programs have been adopted. I have also seen it in science centers with an integrated course curriculum near where I live in Connecticut and Massachusetts. But more must be done.

We should not hesitate to look at and adopt other countries' best practices in education wherever possible, as other nations have. In Germany, for example, looking at what other countries were doing led to reforms that included extending the secondary school day to an all-day schedule where it used to end at lunchtime, and replacing the standard five-year university degree with a two-year/three-year degree system similar to the U.S. bachelor's/master's degree programs. In the first instance, academic scores improved when the all-day schedule was implemented; and in the second instance, it reduced German drop-out rates and gave students more flexibility in determining when to enter the workforce.

---

[136] National Science Board, *Science and Engineering Indicators: 2010* (Arlington, VA: National Science Foundation, January 2010).

Maintaining Leadership in Innovation

Which country will be the first to commercialize an affordable source of renewable energy…or land a human on Mars…or create complex, fully-formed inanimate objects from basic particles?

The answer is: whichever country does the most to support innovation.

Innovation is the "D" end of "R&D," and it has always been a key element of America's economic strength. This will be even truer in the future. Now that services have replaced manufacturing as the leading proportion of GDP, our economy will rely more heavily than ever before on innovation to support our knowledge-based industries in finance, healthcare, technology, and other industries.

America has been a global innovation magnet for decades, thanks to a variety of cultural, financial and technological advantages that we possess. These include a strong university system, openness to new ideas, the willingness to accept failure as a necessary part of taking big risks, rich venture capital markets, and a highly skilled workforce.

But, as I discussed in the last chapter, America's lead in innovation has narrowed discernibly in recent years against competitors in Asia and Europe. That is primarily because these other countries are investing like never before – in education, research facilities, business incubators and start-up funding – at the same time America is scaling back.

To maintain America's leadership in innovation we not only need to invest more in basic science and engineering education, but also in the important applied research that focuses on commercializing advanced technologies and processes into marketable goods and services. Through a combination of private and public initiatives, we need to increase funding for research labs, scientists and technical staffs, as well as to provide start-up money for new enterprises.

When I was the Chair of Connecticut's Technology Transfer Advisory Board, I was deeply engaged in these types of initiatives. In fact, part of my mandate was identifying promising but underfunded research taking place in universities and corporations and working with government and university officials, corporate executives and local business leaders to identify policies and funding sources that would allow such research to be commercialized. Similarly, as Vice Chairman of the Commission for Educational Technology for the State of Connecticut, I was involved in creating policies that would allow recently commercialized technologies to be effectively distributed to schools throughout the state to improve our children's educational opportunities.

A few companies have taken steps to increase their commitment to commercializing innovation. Recently, for example, a consortium of five chip manufacturers, including IBM and Intel, announced a $4.4 billion plan to build a nanotechnology research venture in New York aimed at improving silicon yields and chip processing speeds. And Nike announced plans to set up a Sustainable Business and Innovation Lab to provide venture capital funding for start-ups in alternative energy technologies and efficient manufacturing practices.

But in general, growth in corporate R&D spending – which accounts for almost two-thirds of overall global R&D spending – as a percentage of sales has been virtually flat for over a decade.[137] At the same time, many companies fail to successfully commercialize the research that they do invest in. A great example of this is how the Xerox Palo Alto Research Center (PARC) failed to capitalize on many of its pioneering computer innovations – which included laser printing, graphical user interfaces and the Ethernet communications standard – in the 1970s and 1980s. Furthermore, American companies in recent years have

---

[137] Barry Jaruzelski and Kevin Dehoff, "The Global Innovation 1000: How the Top Innovators Keep Winning," *strategy+business magazine*, Booz & Company, Issue 61, Winter 2010.

been investing significantly more of their R&D budget overseas – in countries like China and South Korea – than they have been investing in U.S. research facilities.[138] To counter this trend, some experts have proposed ideas like increased business R&D tax credits for investments in domestic research initiatives.

Federal programs also used to be more avid supporters of applied research than they are today. For example, research funding from the Department of Defense and NASA between the 1960s and the 1980s led to major commercial developments in materials science, chip design, satellites, and aeronautics. Other research initiatives from the Defense Department led directly to the development of the Internet. But in recent years, when innovation is more important than ever, the Federal Government has been spending less on R&D as a percentage of GDP than it did during the 1950s.[139] And with calls for reducing the Federal budget, more cuts seem likely in the future.

Figure 30 - U.S. R&D Spending as Percent of GDP, 1954-2008

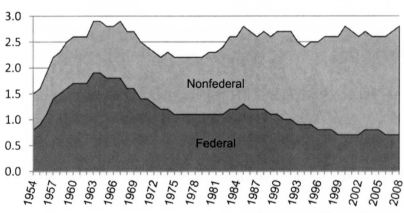

Source: National Science Foundation

---

[138] Barry Jaruzelski and Kevin Dehoff, "Beyond Borders: The Global Innovation 1000," *strategy+business magazine*, Booz & Company, Issue 61, Winter 2008.

[139] National Science Foundation, Division of Science Resources Statistics, *National Patterns of R&D Resources: 2008 Update*, 2010.

Another macro trend that needs to be addressed to maintain America's edge in innovation concerns U.S. immigration policies. As noted earlier in this book, the talents and energies of immigrants have been responsible for some of our most important innovations and our most successful companies. We need to ensure that our immigration policies continue to draw talented and ambitious people from around the world, and allow them to prosper in this country, just as we continue to find better ways to employ our own people.

One way of encouraging immigration would be to ease the visa process for students and entrepreneurs who want to come to the U.S., and make it more attractive for them to remain in the U.S. rather than go home to companies in countries that compete with us. We should seek out and welcome the world's best and brightest, integrate them fully into our culture and our economy, and encourage them to succeed.

America lost its lead in venture capital funding as a percent of GDP to the 15 nations of the European Union in 2009.[140] Perhaps by reinforcing our innovation infrastructure and attracting new talent, we will recapture our lead and re-channel venture capital that is now flowing to overseas businesses back into domestic research facilities, business incubators, and early stage ventures.

Maintaining Leadership in Entrepreneurism

In 1925, it was Calvin Coolidge who said, "The chief business of the American people is business."[141] This sentiment has never been as meaningful as it is today. Our unemployment rate has been stuck at around 9% for over two years, businesses are holding unprecedented

---

[140] Robert D. Atkinson and Scott M. Andes, *The Atlantic Century II: Benchmarking EU & U.S. Innovation and Competiveness* (Washington, DC: The Information Technology and Innovation Foundation, July 2011).

[141] Calvin Coolidge, Speech to the American Society of Newspaper Editors, Washington, DC, January 17, 1925.

amounts of cash because they are fearful of hiring or investing in an uncertain economy, and many banks are reluctant to take risks lending to small businesses. Clearly, it is time to figure out how we can get the economy moving again.

Most economists agree that the best way to create jobs in the U.S. is to invest in new businesses and to innovate within existing ones. We have already talked about innovation, but what can be done to promote new business formation and small business growth?

I think there are three areas we need to focus on. First, we need to make sure that we shape our tax policy so that it does not thwart business formation. High taxes discourage entrepreneurism by eliminating the rewards for entrepreneurial effort and taking risks. If we want new businesses to help our economy, we need to incentivize these new businesses, not punish them.

Thomas Jefferson envisioned, "A wise and frugal government which shall restrain men from injuring one another, shall leave them otherwise free to regulate their own pursuits of industry and improvement, and shall not take from the mouth of labor the bread it has earned."[142] This, to me, sums up the approach that should be guiding our tax policy.

Second, we need to provide capital to help small businesses get started and grow. I already mentioned how I was involved in arranging funding for small businesses so that their technologies could be used to advance educational opportunities in the State of Connecticut. But that was just one initiative, and much more can and must be done. Small businesses have been responsible for 65% of net new jobs over the past 17 years and employ just over half of all private sector employees.[143] It is clear to

---

[142] Thomas Jefferson, First Inaugural Address, Washington, DC, March 4, 1801.

[143] Brian Headd, *An Analysis of Small Business and Jobs* (Washington, DC: U.S. Small Business Administration, March 2010).

me that they will be unable to continue fulfilling this role if government policies and risk-averse banks make it hard for small businesses to access the funds needed to finance growth.

Research by the Raddon Financial Group found that 48% of small businesses that used large banks agreed or strongly agreed with the statement that "Credit standards have become too tight – it is difficult to get a loan."[144] The 2010 Year-End Economic Report by the National Small Business Association supports Raddon's findings, stating that one-third of small businesses could not access the financing they required, and 18% said that as a result, they could not finance increased sales.

Another example is a small business lending program launched by the Treasury Department that came and went in 2011, having disbursed only $4 billion of its $30 billion in available funds to businesses. Two major reasons cited for the lending program's failure were: lending standards were too high and the lending process was too cumbersome. (A third reason was lack of small business demand due to reduced consumer spending.) The message seems clear: we must provide creditworthy small businesses with access to more funds, more easily if we want them to continue producing jobs and invigorating the American economy.

The third area we need to focus on to spur entrepreneurism in America is right-sizing our regulatory framework for business. We need to recognize that there are important differences – in resources, markets served and overall business model – between America's vast number of small businesses and the relatively small number of major corporations.

Today, there are 4,226 federal regulations in the pipeline, 845 of which affect small business. In 2010 alone, 224 "economically

---

[144] Raddon Financial Group. *Fall 2011 National Small Business Research*, October 2011.

significant" rules – those costing the economy $100 million or more – were issued, an increase of 22% over 2009 and the highest number recorded since the government began keeping count. [145]

All of this regulation, obviously, distracts businesses from serving their customers and doing what they do best. And it affects small businesses much more than large ones. To be precise, complying with government regulations costs small firms with fewer than 20 employees $2,830 more on a per employee basis than it costs firms with 500 or more employees, according to the U.S. Small Business Administration.[146]

As Sen. Susan Collins of Maine put it in a recent address, "We need a time out from excessive regulations so that America can get back to work." She added, "Over-regulation is hurting our economy; unfortunately, the problem is only growing worse."[147]

One way to deal with this problem, suggested by the Kauffman Foundation, a non-profit group devoted to promoting entrepreneurship, is to subject all major rules to a thorough cost-benefit analysis before they can be considered. This will help to eliminate needlessly broad or expensive fixes to problems that may not warrant extensive regulation. Along with this, the Foundation suggests that all major rules should have a defined expiration date – perhaps 10 years from their enactment – and would need to be reevaluated before they could be extended. This would allow for a more thorough public examination of the rules' actual impact on business and force too-costly regulations to be replaced.

---

[145] Clyde Wayne Crews, Jr., *Ten Thousand Commandments: An Annual Snapshot of the Federal Regulatory State* (Washington, DC: Competitive Enterprise Institute, April 18, 2011).

[146] Nicole V. Crain and W. Mark Crain, "The Impact of Regulatory Costs on Small Firms," *Small Business Research Summary*, September 2010.

[147] Susan Collins, GOP Weekly Address, Washington, DC, September 24, 2011.

Revitalizing our Financial Institutions

Another important step toward reviving the American Dream and rebuilding the American economy is restoring confidence in our banks and our financial system. As one journalist put it recently, "In ordinary times, confidence is mostly just a consequence of fundamental factors in the economy – revenue, interest rates, employment statistics. In troubled times such as these, it can become the tail that wags the dog."[148]

The American financial system has been subjected to numerous shocks over the past three years and is still absorbing the impact of the various fixes we have prescribed. In the meantime, our financial institutions are struggling to fulfill their role as lubricants of the economy. As America watches them struggle, our faith in these institutions has eroded. A recent Gallup Poll found that a record high 36% of Americans lacked confidence in banks. [149]

To restore health to our financial system, we first need to work our way out of the mortgage mess, and the quicker the better. We need to do a better job of containing risk and ensuring adequate capitalization to prevent future meltdowns, which is what the Dodd-Frank bill is supposed to do. We need to restore lending to creditworthy borrowers to get the economy moving again.

Most importantly, we need to actively support both large and small financial institutions, recognizing the unique role that each plays. In this regard, we must take the same approach toward policy and regulation as with small businesses – adopting policies that clearly differentiate the risks and business models between large and small banks, and ensuring that we don't penalize one to protect the other.

---

[148] Peter Coy, "The Confidence-builder in Chief," *Bloomberg Businessweek*, September 19, 2011.

[149] Dennis Jacobe, *Record-High 36% of Americans Lack Confidence in Banks*, Gallup, June 24, 2011.

Specifically, we need to be mindful of the unintended consequences of regulations like Dodd-Frank that make it hard for small financial institutions to survive. In chapter 3, I discussed how, in the wake of the financial crisis, government policies that were designed to de-risk the financial system, stabilize the economy and protect the consumer did none of these things while undermining the community-based financial institutions that are a key source of economic strength.

Dodd-Frank raised compliance costs, reduced fee income, and imposed more stringent capital requirements on small institutions that had very little to do with the financial crisis. As a consequence, it made it harder for small banks and credit unions to fulfill their economic role serving homeowners, small businesses, and people who might otherwise be unbanked or underbanked in communities across America.

In financial services, as in all industries, competition is necessary to meet different market needs, spur innovation and keep prices under control. That is why preserving America's community banks and credit unions is so essential. If we let smaller institutions fail, the hegemony of large banks will most likely create vast numbers of unserved and underserved consumers and businesses, less differentiation of services and institutions, and higher prices for basic services such as checking accounts, ATMs, online banking and debit cards. We saw a preview of this in the fall of 2011, when large banks, including Bank of America and Wells Fargo, tried to impose new fees on debit cards and instituted higher fees for services such as overdraft protection and returned checks. After considerable public outcry and depositors threatening to close their accounts, most banks reversed the new fee policies.

Banking in a Time of Over-Regulation

By FRANK KEATING, President and CEO of the American Bankers Association

What's the key to stimulating our economy? Consider a conversation I had recently with a banker in Nebraska. For the first time, he said, his bank now devotes more work hours to compliance than to lending. Specifically, he has 1.2 employees on compliance for every one employee focused on lending and bringing in business.

Imagine a manufacturing company that deployed more than half of its work force as Occupational Health and Safety Administration (OSHA) compliance officers. Such a company would be unable to grow, let alone contribute to broader economic growth.

Yet banks across the country are feeling a similar pull on resources as the Dodd-Frank Act is implemented. Already federal regulators have issued 4,870 Federal Register pages of proposed or final rules affecting banks. Many more are still to come—for a grand total of more than 240 rules. And that's on top of about 50 new or expanded regulations unrelated to Dodd-Frank that banks have had to absorb over the past two years.

Managing this mountainous regulatory burden is a significant challenge for a bank of any size. but for the median-sized bank—with 37 employees—it's overwhelming. The cost of regulatory compliance as a share of operating expenses is two and a half times greater for small banks than for large banks.

Small-business owners can relate. A recent National Federation of Independent Business poll found that owners' top concerns

(continued on next page)

are poor sales, taxes and government regulation or red tape—not access to credit, as those who want to blame banks for the stalled economic recovery suggest. In fact, 92% of small-business owners reported either that all their credit needs were met or that they were not interested in borrowing.

More regulation doesn't necessarily make consumers safer, banks stronger, or the economy healthier. More regulation—if it's not smart regulation—can have the opposite effect, chilling growth and driving up prices.

Americans understand this. In fact, when asked in a recent poll by the Tarrance Group who they believe is most affected by the costs that federal regulations create—consumers, business or the federal government itself—six in 10 voters said "consumers."

Better regulation can lead to growth and improved service. A state that can process a new branch application in six weeks, for example, will serve its population and economy better than one that drags the process out for two years.

While better regulation is not synonymous with less regulation, there's no doubt our federal code is rife with outdated, confusing or counterproductive rules that would fail any cost-benefit test. President Obama's regulatory reduction initiative, in which he asked government agencies to scour their rulebooks for policies that might be hampering business efforts to grow and create jobs, was a good start in exposing rules to such a test.

But the agencies, as if unsure whether the president wanted substantive relief or the appearance of it, were far too timid in their response. The pace and complexity of new regulations

(continued on next page)

coming online will quickly overwhelm and obscure the nips and tucks that the agencies agreed to this month.

What's needed is a bold initiative that reverses the trend of over-regulation and frees the private sector to do its job. We need an approach to regulation that will ensure fundamental protection of consumers, the environment and other concerns without bogging businesses down in red tape or chilling expansion with threats of additional rules and harsh penalties. Bankers, for instance, need to know that they can exercise discretion and make a loan to a customer they know well without fear of reprisal from an overly cautious examiner.

Solutions should be government-enabled, not government-funded. That's how growth will come to Main Street—and not just to the federal regulatory agencies, where employment has surged 13% since 2009.

Lee Iacocca once described his formula for success as hiring brighter people than himself and then getting out of their way. Government would do well to follow this advice.

America is full of bright, energetic businessmen and women. Entrepreneurs are eager to innovate, expand, hire and sell, if government would just get out of the way.

In addition to what the government can do to ensure the survival and health of America's community-based financial institutions, there is much that our community-based institutions can do for themselves. I believe that community-based financial institutions must recognize that the financial services environment has radically changed due to industry consolidation, expanded consumer demand for new modes of interaction with financial institutions (through channels such as the Internet, mobile, direct deposit and so on), and the threat of financial services commoditization and consumerization, in which empowered customers shop around for financial services and meet their needs through multiple providers, as with any consumer product.

To avoid becoming commoditized, smaller financial institutions must be clear about their role in this new environment and the qualities that make them unique. There is no longer any mystery about basic financial services products. Increasingly well-informed consumers are able to understand and compare products quickly and easily using readily available information. Being clear about their unique commitment to communities and their strong community affinity, their service- and relationship-based culture, and their focus on providing basic financial products will allow smaller financial institutions to compete better and fill an essential community need.

At the same time, smaller financial institutions must adopt new ways of working to compete in today's environment by taking advantage of technology and collaboration to increase their efficiency and better serve the needs of their customers and members. In an age of Google, mobile applications and App stores, it is astounding that many institutions still operate with systems that rely on programming languages, technologies and practices that were designed as long as forty years ago. These are clearly no longer adequate for today's demands, and nearly every other industry has long since abandoned and moved on from such "legacy" technologies. Holding on to antiquated systems may also be what's preventing smaller financial institutions from taking advantage of opportunities to collaborate and innovate together in ways that would allow them to better compete against the scale and volume benefits of larger banks.

Making Your Differences More Clear

A lot of people probably don't realize that America is the one of the few countries whose banking system consists of a relatively small group of large national and regional financial institutions along with a vast number of small, locally-run community financial institutions. In many parts of the world, there is no such choice; all communities are served solely by large national banks.

But availability and choice are not the only things that make community-based financial institutions unique. Because of their size and asset base, community-based financial institutions are intrinsically limited in the variety of services they can offer. As a result, they tend to focus on meeting the most important needs of the people they serve, such as housing, autos, funding small businesses, and providing basic credit. What they lack in breadth, however, they more than make up for in depth by developing a special closeness with the members of their communities.

The people who run community-based financial institutions typically live and work directly within their local communities – in other words, they know and routinely interact with the neighbors who are their customers or members – and they make their financial decisions locally. This in-depth familiarity with the local community's people, places and points of view, along with high levels of personalized service, are the small financial institutions' greatest strengths, and consumers repeatedly attest to this once they have had experience doing business with a community bank or credit union.

Community-based financial institutions also play a vital role in providing financial services to demographic groups that otherwise might be underserved by larger institutions. This includes rural communities and people with low to moderate incomes, as well as small businesses and consumers across all communities who value human as opposed to computer- and policy-driven decision making.

Unfortunately, all of these differentiating strengths can be easily overlooked by the consumer who has not had the experience of banking with a smaller, local institution or who is simply shopping around for financial services. More and more, consumers have come to view financial services – such as checking accounts, online banking, mortgage and business lending, etc. – as commodities, with no significant difference among providers.

This is one area where smaller banks can do a much better job of helping themselves and helping consumers, by making their differences clear and de-commoditizing the financial services experience. It is also an area where smaller financial institutions can take advantage of the opportunity to increase their difference by further enhancing their customer and member relationships. And, ironically enough, the key to promoting closer personal relationships rests squarely on technology.

Banking has long been one of the biggest users of technology, accounting for nearly half of all technology spending by industry. Banking was also once a leading source of technological innovation, much of it stemming from the need to handle ever-larger numbers of transactions with greater efficiency. But as computing technology evolved and effectively solved the transaction processing need, many banks became complacent about their core enterprise processing systems. That is probably why many banks are now operating with the oldest enterprise technology of any industry.

Of course, a lot has changed in the decades since most of these banking systems were put in place. Most importantly, banking evolved from being a transaction-centric business into a person-centric one. As a result, many banks that are still using yesterday's transaction- and account-oriented processing systems to meet current banking needs are finding themselves strategically challenged. Trying to "make do," they have added successive layers of middleware to bridge the gap between their older transaction-based technologies and today's relationship-oriented applications, but this has often resulted in hugely complex and inefficient systems that are expensive and difficult to maintain.

To remain competitive and strengthen their differences, community-based financial institutions can no longer fall back on outdated and unwieldy approaches to their core banking systems. Despite the initial cost, they must finally break free of the stranglehold they are locked into with needlessly limited and proprietary systems, and invest in a newer class of enterprise software that is specifically designed to manage relationships, increase flexibility, reduce costs and enable new services, as well as handle the full range of financial transactions.

An American Dream and Revolution...

Achieving the American Dream has never been easy. But hard-working, industrious people have always found a way to use whatever resources were at hand to reshape their lives and realize their dreams. The financial services industry is on the cusp of change, reforming itself to deal with government regulations and competitive pressures. We're also reinventing the way we do business to better serve our accountholders.

Because of regulatory changes, Redstone and other financial institutions have seen a dramatic increase in customer service

(continued on next page)

---

calls related to overdrafts and non-payment of transactions. This change in public policy created an obstacle – an impediment to serving our members. It was taking our staff an unacceptable amount of time to gather information and serve accountholders. Our IT developers quickly began to explore a solution.

Using a suite of software tools called DNAcreator, our team developed a technology solution that reduced call time by 75 percent. Technology gave something precious back to our members: their time. It is also making us more productive, efficient and profitable.

Although we developed this innovation to benefit our members, modern technology is allowing us to share this solution with our global community of banks and credit unions through Open Solutions' online DNAappstore. Financial Institutions anywhere in the world can download and use this and other solutions to serve their accountholders.

Redstone developers and others are now thinking differently about how they create solutions. They're not just solving problems for their own organizations – they're developing applications that will benefit an open marketplace. This ability to make positive change will help financial institutions recruit individuals that want to use their talent to benefit banks and credit unions around the world – and this will lead to revolutionary change.

Reforming a business model and recasting an industry certainly leads to obstacles. Taking them on is what it means to be an innovator, and a leader.

Joseph Newberry, President and CEO
Redstone Federal Credit Union

Today's far more capable enterprise software is built on powerful relational database systems; more advanced, flexible and adaptable programming tools; and collaborative and distributed technologies.

With their relational design, such systems make the person – not the transaction – the fundamental unit around which all data is organized and structured. This basic difference makes it possible for financial institutions to rapidly capture and deliver an unlimited amount of information about a person, business or other entity right at the point of service. It also makes it possible to capture and act upon the complex and changing relationships that define each person or entity in the database, without storing redundant information. In short, relational systems offer a more flexible, efficient and useful way to understand the people and relationships that are the heart of the financial business.

Modern enterprise software is also built on open rather than proprietary standards to take advantage of faster, more sophisticated and lower cost hardware architectures, and to allow modular software components – for things like customer relationship management (CRM), online and mobile banking, profitability analysis by person, and so forth – to integrate seamlessly with the enterprise processing system. This openness allows institutions to choose whatever hardware, operating software and components meet their strategic needs, at a lower cost. It also makes it possible for a single base of programming code to adapt to the needs of a wide range of businesses, rather than the old approach of packaging essentially identical functionality into completely separate applications.

Finally, a modern enterprise system incorporates collaborative and distributive technologies that allow institutions to share innovation with each other at a lower cost. In essence, this means giving financial institutions the tools not only to enhance and modify their own systems, but also to share their enhancements with others, who can put them to work in their own businesses.

If smaller banks and credit unions expect to continue serving their role as the financial service providers of choice for their communities – with their unique focus on personal relationships – it is essential that they adopt the open standards and relationship-based technologies that allow them to do so. I can't think of any other industry that is trying to meet the consumer needs of the 21st century with enterprise technology that in many cases dates back to the 1960s and 1970s, is over-specialized and is designed for a completely different business model. The bar has been raised on banking systems; extending the life of fundamentally outdated technology can only serve to make smaller banks less nimble, less profitable and less able to fulfill their mandate in supporting the American Dream.

While upgrading to a modern enterprise system may seem costly and challenging, it actually has become much easier in recent years as software companies develop more efficient processes and tools to manage the job. Even more to the point, community-based financial institutions must consider the cost of not upgrading their technology infrastructure, which will be reflected in higher operating expenses, increased regulatory compliance costs, and reduced levels of service, placing them at a severe competitive disadvantage.

Embracing Collaboration

Collaboration is another area in which community-based financial institutions can better adapt to the changing financial services environment and ensure their long-term viability. By collaborating with other community banks and credit unions, smaller institutions will find new ways to accelerate innovation, reduce costs, strengthen interpersonal relationships and advance the interests of the entire industry.

Community-based financial institutions have seen the enemy and it is not each other. Through collaboration, they will be better able to work and compete as one, leveraging the immense strength and influence they collectively possess. This is not a far-fetched or radical idea. After all, smaller institutions share many of the same processes and face many of the same challenges. The good news is that there are numerous opportunities for working together, and sharing the cost and delivery of commodity-type services among several institutions.

Sharing services is a simple model that eliminates redundancy and waste. It allows each participant to lower their individual costs while operating more flexibly and efficiently. Many IT and back-office support services make excellent candidates for a shared service model. For example, routine and non-differentiating tasks such as image processing, mortgage processing, credit checks, payment processing and certain accounting services could all be easily shared by multiple institutions, rather than duplicated at each.

Of course, the bonus for spending less time on non-differentiating tasks is that it allows institutions to devote more time and resources to the tasks that are differentiating – such as providing more personalized service or developing innovative offerings.

Opportunities for collaboration exist not only among other financial institutions, but also among vendors and partners. Many banks and credit unions have been able to add convenience and save money by sharing ATM networks and pooling their call centers. Others have begun sharing branches, handling their competitors' transactions in exchange for the convenience of establishing a new branch presence. Financial institutions have even banded together to establish buying consortia to take advantage of volume discounts on supplies and other materials. There is no end to the opportunities available – from mobile providers, insurance companies, software providers and anyone else in the sphere of influence – once banks adopt the spirit of collaboration.

Collaboration isn't just focused on services anymore, either. Today, it is possible for banks to collaborate globally, sharing ideas and developing new applications to enhance their business. Again, this is one of the advantages of moving away from a transaction-oriented architecture to a person-centric one. When banking systems are designed and built around the individual, it is possible to share applications, systems and technology innovations with other financial institutions around the world, and even service the same person regardless of where they are and what products they use.

I am proud to say that it was my own software company, Open Solutions, that pioneered this concept just last year when we introduced a revolutionary collaborative ecosystem known as the DNAappstore for our DNA core processing system. The DNAappstore is a unique online collective we invented where banks and credit unions can learn about, shop for, and immediately download innovative solutions from developers around the globe to enhance their DNA core processing system. It is also a place where financial institutions, independent developers or vendor partners can easily access the tools needed to develop new applications for DNA (using the free DNAcreator development suite), and share them among the collective through the DNAappstore.

The big idea behind the DNAappstore is to democratize technology development by allowing clients, independent developers and vendors around the world to exchange ideas and collaborate on common business problems to provide solutions that will advance the success and competitiveness of community-based institutions. This global, collaborative network allows everyone in the financial institution community to share their ideas for free or sell the apps that they create in a marketplace that ensures quality though a rigorous application certification process. American Banker called the DNAappstore "mind bending," and Bank Technology News cited the DNAappstore when it named Open Solutions to its recent list of "Top Ten Tech Companies to Watch."

The final area in which collaboration is essential for community-based financial institutions is in advancing the common interests of their industry. I have said many times that community financial institutions need to make their differences more clear. This is true both for individual institutions when speaking to their markets, and for all community banks and credit unions in the aggregate when speaking to their legislators.

The message of how Main Street banks are different from Wall Street banks, how smaller institutions can uniquely meet the financial needs of their communities, how personal knowledge of your customers, members and communities serves the country's economic interests… all these messages and more need to be communicated to the public, as well as to legislators and constituents who just don't seem to "get it."

Most importantly, in areas of regulation, community-based financial institutions need to speak loudly and in a single voice to be heard over Wall Street's mighty lobbying din. Community banks and credit unions represent 98% of all banks in America. If they were viewed as a single entity, it would be the largest single financial institution in the country. (Through collaboration, this scale could even grow to include financial institutions from around the world.) It is time to pull together and leverage this power – through our legislatures and grassroots community outreach – to ensure that the needs of smaller institutions get the same representation and attention that larger institutions do.

Banks and credit unions have already proven that they can work together toward a common goal. Consider the collaborative effort by the Credit Union National Association, the American Bankers

Association and other groups who pulled together recently to call for a "stop and study" delay in the implementation of the Durbin Amendment. Although the initiative did not succeed in delaying the bill, it represented the kind of collaboration that will be increasingly important to ensure the future of community-based financial institutions.

Adapting to a changed environment, taking personal responsibility for our future, restoring competitiveness and innovation, and rebuilding confidence in our institutions are all essential steps along the path to reviving the American Dream. All that is needed is the courage to take the first steps, and the determination to stay the course until the job is done.

6: Leading the Next Comeback

*"Innovation distinguishes between
a leader and a follower."*
Steve Jobs

In 1985, a high-flying California tech company that had amassed an enviable track record of successes unexpectedly stumbled. It saw a key geographic market defect en masse to its leading rival. The company introduced a major new product only to have it summarily rejected by its intended customers. Sales slowed, and the company's stock price sank to half of its prior year's value. A second new product introduction started off with promise but quickly lost momentum. Business steadily declined and a raft of layoffs and management shakeups ensued – culminating in the ousting of the president and CEO.

Over the next 12 years, the company diligently managed to more than triple sales, but consistently failed to boost profits. Eventually, the company's financial situation became so dire that it was more than $1 billion in the red and seemed to be on the verge of going out of business. It was forced to accept a $150 million loan from a competitor just to stay afloat. The year was 1997 and the company in distress was Apple Computer. Microsoft was the savior that offered up the life-saving loan.

Fast-forward to today, and Apple has grown to be the most valuable company in the U.S. Its market cap is now more than one and one half times the size of Microsoft's. Its customers are among the most loyal of any in history – lining up for hours to buy each new iGadget the company introduces – and its products are the envy of marketers, designers and electronics makers around the world.

It is no exaggeration to say that Apple staged one of the great comebacks in the annals of business. And, according to most sources, the resurgence was driven almost exclusively by the focus, dedication and visionary leadership of Apple CEO, Steve Jobs, who after being unceremoniously ousted from his position, returned to rescue the company during its most troubled times.

Figure 31 - Apple and Microsoft, Market Capitalization, 2001-2011

($ Billions)

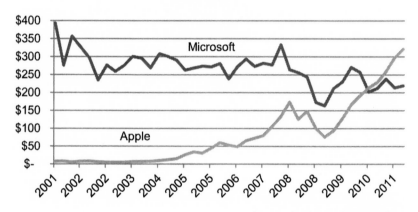

Source: Apple Inc. & Microsoft Inc.

America is at an inflection point that is in some ways reminiscent of Apple in 1997. We have a great "product" that consists of our political and economic systems, our infrastructure, our educational institutions, our culture and our people. What we haven't done is to maximize the social rate of return from our investment, as its framework has become increasingly disconnected from – and irrelevant to – the realities of a globally interconnected world. The task before us is to make our product relevant again – capable of delivering new opportunities for people to improve their standard of living, new ways to achieve economic growth, and new strategies for sustaining our advantages in the future.

We have a choice: we can become progressively marginalized on the global stage or engineer our own great comeback, recapturing the energy and vitality that has made America exceptional and helps us remain a beacon of hope for the world. I believe that our place in history will be defined as much by what happens next as what has come before, and by those people who are leading the way.

American Innovation Can Come from Anywhere...

Innovation is a hallmark of the American Dream and I take great pride playing a small, but important role in helping drive that creativity. To deliver the next big idea, companies in our home market of Silicon Valley must continue attracting creative genius to their organizations, and the next great engineer or scientist that calls our community home could come from anywhere in the world.

Silicon Valley is America's high-tech hub for innovation, research and development. Global firms like Google, Genentech, Facebook and others are constantly recruiting talent from abroad. All too often, however, these highly sought out inventors can't say yes to the job because a big bank has said no to their home mortgage application.

A local biotech firm was courting an eminent scientist from Switzerland who wanted to join the company and move his entire family to California. Since he wasn't a U.S. citizen, he didn't have a social security number, a record of earning a living in America, or a credit score. The big banks looked no further and denied his mortgage application. That's bad for the company, our marketplace and hurts America's ability to be an innovative leader in the global economy.

(continued on next page)

> Our credit union approved the loan to the scientist because sometimes you need to ignore rigid mortgage formulas and create different, yet conservative ways for great thinkers to make their home in America. We're playing a special part in helping America grow its knowledge-based economy by lending to a segment of the population that is overlooked by large banks.
>
> People come from all over the world to experience the American Dream. It may be to develop that next great idea, own a home with a white picket fence – or both, if we have anything to do with it.
>
> *Joan Opp, President and CEO*
> *Stanford Federal Credit Union*
>
>

We live in a much different world today than we did 50 years ago. We have evolved from a manufacturing economy to a knowledge economy in which ideas and innovation have become the new currency of exchange. We have created a truly global marketplace built on a network of technological, cultural and financial interconnections with other nations and economies. As we have seen, American ideals have been widely adopted and often improved upon by nations everywhere. At the same time, we have seen financial and political crises erupt around the world resulting from the massive changes that are taking place.

It is important to remember that major changes invariably create dislocations as old models give way to new, and that much of the social and economic pain we are experiencing today may be the result of such dislocations. In the past, America has always adapted to major changes and remained a bulwark of personal, religious, political and economic freedom. While today's dislocations may not appear as great as others in our history – after all, there are no visible signs of strife, such as entrenched poverty, persecution or national hostilities – I consider them to be the most significant ones we will ever face, if only because it will be extraordinarily difficult to regain our preeminence if we ever lose it.

One key to navigating the current dislocations is maintaining our commitment to the original meaning of the American Dream. The time has come to clearly focus our behaviors, policies and expectations on providing equal opportunities for success, rather than aiming for an equal distribution of prosperity. We must regain a sense of earning "our fair share," relying on ambition, determination and individual effort for our achievements, rather than expecting to get something for nothing.

On a broader scale, we will need to recalibrate our standards for the world as it is today. Clinging to outdated beliefs and making incremental changes to fundamentally outmoded policies, behaviors and expectations have caused us to fall out of step with our peers and our times. We need to analyze our policies and beliefs, abandon what isn't working and adopt completely new models to guide our future aspirations.

Our challenge today is analogous to what I described in the previous chapter for financial institutions that try to meet the needs of radically changed market requirements by applying layers of "fixes" to fundamentally outdated technologies. This only serves to reduce their agility, increase their costs and make them less competitive, rather than more so. America must not fall into the same trap. We must recapture our leadership by turning our attention to the needs of the next century, identifying and overhauling out-of-date policies and behaviors, and implementing major changes in key areas of our socio-economic policy.

Redefining American Education

In education, Americans must focus on meeting new social and economic realities rather than incremental improvements in entrenched curricula and teaching methods. In the past, Americans developed the skills needed to become masters of business administration and leaders of the manufacturing economy. In the 21st century, we must develop our scientific and technical skills to become masters of innovation and leaders of the knowledge economy.

Considering the explosion of information that is available from the Internet, knowing how and where to access information is far more important than possessing that information. Where our teaching methods encourage rote memorization rather than creative problem solving, we need to rethink whether these methods are viable.

Similarly, if the standards and achievement levels being set by other nations are higher than our own, we should be learning from and adopting their best practices to upgrade our teaching methods and raising our standards, rather than simply measuring against our own historical benchmarks. We should strive to attain academic performance that rivals what students in countries like China and Finland have achieved, particularly in the areas of math and science. With open eyes and open minds, we can ensure that our educational policies and institutions remain relevant to – and ahead of – the times.

I think it is important that we also demand a better return on our educational investment. According to the OECD, America is among the top-ten countries when it comes to spending per pupil for primary and secondary education.[150] What we need to do now is to tie public educational spending to quantifiable academic results at all levels,

---

[150] Organisation for Economic Co-operation and Development, *OECD Education Database*, 2011.

while offering support to those at both the lowest and highest levels of achievement. In higher education, we should make sure college costs and the economic benefits of higher education are closely aligned. The fact is, we do not need a generation of graduates with insufficient skills, unmanageable student loan debts, and few opportunities for employment.

In secondary education, we need to focus on quality, not quantity, to ensure that students are prepared to excel in more rigorous and relevant college education programs. America has relatively high college and high school graduation rates, but we clearly lag behind our global peers in terms of skills and knowledge gained, which again puts us at a competitive disadvantage.

Part of the solution to this problem involves raising the standards and economic rewards for educators to attract those who possess the qualifications and knowledge needed to educate and inspire our students. At the same time, we should put assessments and policies in place to raise accountability among teachers and winnow out the underperformers.

Quality versus quantity should be part of the agenda for higher education, as well. To compete globally in the scientific, engineering and technical industries that matter in the 21st century, we need creative thinkers with a much greater technical literacy than many graduates possess today. Google could never have evolved without its founders' knowledge and experience in mathematics, and Intel could never have developed advanced microprocessors without a firm grounding in materials science. By lacking the knowledge to fully understand today's technologies, we are unable to imagine better ways of doing things that lie at the heart of innovation.

Rebuilding American Housing

America needs to resolve the current mortgage and foreclosure crisis, explore viable alternatives to the super-sized single-family home and maintain meaningful qualification guidelines for mortgages. For at least the past 70 years, homeownership has been a near-sacred part of the American Dream, and for good reason. Homes are an important foundation of building personal wealth and stable communities. But that doesn't mean everyone needs a 4,000-square-foot McMansion with an equally outsized mortgage.

About 3 million homes have been repossessed since the housing boom ended in 2006, and at least one industry expert predicts the number of repossessions could reach 6 million by 2013.[151] Meanwhile, American families have seen trillions of dollars in housing wealth completely disappear since 2008, resulting in countless homeowners walking away from mortgages or refusing to take jobs in new communities because of sinking home values.

It is time to question – as many economists already have – how easily attainable homeownership should be and whether our policies are putting the right people in the right homes. Tougher lending standards and increased documentation requirements are important first steps toward a more rational and sustainable housing market. So is the recognition that people with different financial means must have different and more varied housing choices that allow them to live within their means.

We should not tolerate policies (such as the Community Reinvestment Act of 1977) that encourage irresponsible borrowing to provide housing for American families. Our goal should be to help people affordably meet their long-term housing needs, not to have people

---

[151] Rick Sharga, Senior Vice President at RealtyTrac, in Dan Levy and Prashant Gopal, "Foreclosure Filings in U.S. May Jump 20% From Record 2010 as Crisis Peaks," *Bloomberg*, January 13, 2011.

overextend themselves, accumulate unmanageable debt and end up in foreclosure.

It might even make sense to reconsider whether or not the standard 30-year fixed rate mortgage is the best way for people to pay for their homes. Many other options could be made available that are better suited to our long-term financial health. Again, the issue at hand is short-term affordability versus long-term viability. For comparison's sake, consider that people in many countries save for decades to pay for their homes in cash.

While admittedly the idea of paying cash up-front for a home would probably not work in America, we should remember that the primary reason we enjoy 30-year fixed-rate mortgages at all is due to the role that Fannie Mae and Freddie Mac have played in the secondary mortgage market, buying mortgage obligations from smaller lenders and providing them with the cash to make additional loans.

As America's housing debt and foreclosure problems continue to mount, however, it is clear to me that we probably need a wholesale overhaul of programs like Fannie Mae and Freddie Mac. If we don't abandon these programs altogether, we should at least question the wisdom of allowing them to hold large amounts of subprime and ALT-A mortgages, and allowing the members of their board to be politically appointed. Considering their disproportionate role in the secondary mortgage market, it would also be reasonable to subject these institutions to much greater oversight, whether via the SEC or another regulatory body, and hold their officers accountable for their decisions.

Restoring American Jobs and Entrepreneurism

America must make it easier for entrepreneurs to establish and build the small businesses that create more than 65% of net new jobs in the U.S. on average, while encouraging more distributed and shared workplace alternatives. There are many things we can do to better support entrepreneurism and, thereby, aid job creation.

For starters, we can give entrepreneurs greater access to the capital needed to grow their businesses. This means loosening the constraints on community-based financial institutions, which are the primary source of funds for small business lending. This is by far the most important thing we can do to spur small business formation and growth – and the jobs that invariably follow.

Another step we can take is easing taxes and regulations that raise the cost of doing business and distract entrepreneurs from doing what they do best. Today's tax and regulatory policies are needlessly burdensome on smaller business and they discourage entrepreneurs from taking risks and starting new businesses in the U.S.

To support continued innovation, we need to think about increasing university and government spending on basic and applied research in industries of the future, while providing incentives that encourage American companies to invest more in domestic research facilities. These investments, along with a stronger educational emphasis on technical literacy, are essential to assure America's position as a fountainhead of innovation and economic vitality.

Yet another way to encourage innovation is to radically overhaul our patent system. The current system was designed for a time when we were a manufacturing-based economy and no longer serves the purpose of protecting the rights of the small inventor. Instead, it is being used mostly by large companies to protect and prevent new players from entering established markets, which has the effect of strangling innovation. Our current patent system is also too inefficient to keep up with the volume of applications that today's economy generates. By the same token, we must safeguard our patents and innovations by creating a level global playing field and enforcing stronger international protections for intellectual property, which constitutes a knowledge economy's most valuable assets.

As we think about ways to reduce the hurdles to entrepreneurism, we should simultaneously find ways to support the more flexible and collaborative working arrangements that have resulted from advances in technology and business organization. Having all members of a team in the same physical location simply isn't the way business happens today. We need to encourage and take full advantage of new workplace paradigms, including telecommuting, ad-hoc teams, freelance and shared employment, outsourcing, shared services and cooperation. An important part of this will be improving the availability of high-speed broadband communication, which is as essential to growing the knowledge economy as trains and highways were to the industrial economy.

Finally, we should look at reforming healthcare and tort laws so entrepreneurs are not discouraged from going into business, hiring new workers and taking risks. We should examine whether our immigration policies are designed to attract talented people from other countries and let them remain in the U.S to build businesses or contribute to our economy. And we should look at creating programs to retrain workers with obsolete skills in declining industries so these people can fill jobs and participate in America's knowledge-based economy.

Saving our Main Street Financial Institutions

It has become abundantly clear to me that the American economy cannot move forward until we ensure the health of Main Street and Wall Street banks so that both may continue to facilitate productive economic activity. I have already highlighted the importance of basic credit to the American economy and the role that financial institutions play as the primary lubricant of entrepreneurism. If our financial institutions are to continue fulfilling this important role, we need to recognize the major differences between Main Street and Wall Street financial institutions, encourage each to succeed within its chosen market, and ensure that our policies do not punish one to help the other.

Specifically, we need to re-engineer our financial regulations and policies to address the vastly different resources, capital access options, and business models that separate Main Street and Wall Street banks. This means revising or repealing provisions in the Dodd-Frank Act – such as the capital ratio requirements in the Collins Amendment and the interchange fee limits in the Durbin Amendment – that place unfair financial and compliance burdens upon community-based financial institutions. It is crucial that we allow smaller financial institutions to perform their basic business of lending and investing in their communities without costly and unwarranted government interference.

We also need to place more stringent capital and other requirements on "Too Big to Fail" institutions. For instance, we should limit the types of investments and levels of risk that financial institutions may take on, to prevent investment failures from threatening long-term financial institution viability. We should also consider ways to reduce the largest banks' systemic importance and possibly make them self-insuring, to eliminate the environment that allows them to profit richly from their successes while covering their losses with taxpayer dollars.

Another way to ensure a fairer and more stable financial system is to decouple the direct financial relationship between the ratings agencies and their bank sponsors to eliminate conflicts of interest. This could be accomplished, for example, by establishing a lottery system for assigning bond ratings so that no bank could predetermine which credit rating agency would be responsible for evaluating a given bond offering.

On the topic of fairness, we should seek to find new ways for community-based institutions to raise capital so that they are not wholly dependent on deposits. Large banks have the option of raising capital directly in the financial markets, which can be much less expensive than raising capital from deposits, and this gives the large banks an unfair advantage. We should also consider providing greater flexibility on the types of products that community financial institutions can offer to better meet the needs of their communities and remain competitive with their larger peers.

Community-based financial institutions can do more to help themselves, as well. They can upgrade their technology infrastructure so that they are better prepared to address their current challenges and compete in the emerging, global financial environment. In order for this to become a reality, however, we need to make sure that our regulatory policies aren't biased in favor of outdated technology models that discourage investments in newer and more efficient platforms. Secondly, community-based financial institutions can do a better job of explaining to their constituents how they are different from others, and encourage their constituents to care about and factor these unique differences into the process for selecting a financial institution. Finally, in areas where community-based financial institutions are not different, they must find ways of working with others to share costs so that they operate more efficiently and position themselves to compete long term.

Refocusing American Public Policy

My general view and recommendation, which extends to all areas of American policy, is that we must carefully consider the impacts and consequences of legislative proposals for all constituents while ensuring that our policies are aligned with the expectations and needs of a sustainable American Dream.

We can – and should – do more to support vital growth initiatives in education, jobs, small business development, immigration, and research to be better prepared for the world we live in today. We must avoid the temptation to slash government spending and incentives in the places and times when they can do the most good. The best example of this may be supporting businesses and creating jobs in today's recession.

Our public policies should also not encourage unrealistic expectations, but rather aim to produce exceptional opportunities for people who want to take advantage of them. Our policies should serve as a model for private behavior and remain – like our people – adaptable to the times. While I understand the political reasons that we have remained stuck in old belief systems, financial realities make it clear that now is the time to reset our policies on housing and debt while reducing the unsustainable costs of entitlement programs such as social security, Medicare and Medicaid, which inhibit productive economic activity.

We need to eliminate all forms of useless regulation that simply raise costs for businesses, stifle innovation, and lower economic output. The American Dream cannot be achieved if we continue to pump out regulations designed to protect the consumer and stabilize the economy while unintentionally undermining both. Similarly, we must eliminate the kinds of pork-barrel waste (such as the unrelated "additions" to Dodd-Frank) that result in corrupt policy and make a mockery of our legislative process.

We must look to our leaders to be in the vanguard of resetting expectations. They should not be allowed to manipulate the tools of government – such as housing policy or Federal Reserve interest rate policy – to achieve their own political ends. They must, instead, put their political goals and career self-interest aside to fulfill their duties on behalf of the American people. Politicians: this is not the time to ask what America can do for you, but rather what you can do for America. It is time to rise to the challenge of creating jobs, improving education, stabilizing the economy, managing our government debt, and limiting regulations and waste to increase our nation's competitiveness on the global playing field.

The Power of Innovative Leadership

Granted, this is an ambitious plan…and an incomplete one. But it is a starting point for achieving what is needed to break the cycle of economic uncertainty that holds America back from investing in jobs and innovation, inhibits our competitiveness, and degrades our confidence in the future. It is a plan that requires visionary leaders to make it happen – innovators who are willing to take risks and try new things. The great news is, there are numerous examples of people who are already taking the lead in changing America's future.

In education, for example, Salman Khan – an MIT-educated computer scientist, Harvard MBA and former hedge-fund analyst – is an innovator who turned a simple idea for helping his niece with her math homework into a major new approach to educational materials and learning mathematics. Using just a blackboard and simple voice-overs, Khan created a series of videos that walked his niece through the process of understanding difficult mathematics concepts and solving problems.

Khan's back-to-basics approach proved so effective that he decided to create more math videos, which he posted and shared via YouTube. Even with such esoteric titles as "Proof of the Cauchy-Schwarz Inequality," the videos became a kind of viral hit, with some attracting more than 200,000 viewers. Today, Khan heads the Khan

Academy, a diverse online learning community which has become one of the most popular educational sites in the world, with more than 2,300 videos and funding from Google, Bill Gates, and some of the country's leading venture capital firms. Most importantly, his videos are now available not only to online viewers…they have also been incorporated into the math curriculum in school classrooms across the country.

Among entrepreneurs, there are leaders like Shai Agassi – a former executive at a leading enterprise software firm – who put together a team of engineers, government leaders, auto manufacturers, energy companies, banks and others to address one of the major challenges of the 21st century: sustainable transportation. His Silicon Valley company, Better Place, is currently working on technologies to realize the vision of creating a zero-emission vehicle powered by electricity from renewable sources.

In research, there are people like Wes Jackson, a plant geneticist and co-founder of the Kansas-based Land Institute, who is working on discovering ways to transform food staples like wheat, rice and sorghum into perennial crops instead of annuals. His research, if successful, has the potential to radically alter the practice and economics of agriculture, eliminating the need for plowing and replanting fields each year, and reducing the use of fertilizers.

In financial services, innovation has taken hold slowly, but there are clearly opportunities to explore. For instance, who ever imagined we would be able to photograph a check with a smartphone, send the image to a financial institution and have the funds automatically deposited in our account? Or that companies like Payveris would allow us to make direct, person-to-person payments anonymously via the telephone or Internet? Along the same lines, who expected to find their financial institution on Facebook? But the fact is, more and more banks and credit unions have established their presence on social media sites to be closer to where their customers are.

Community-based financial institutions that are the focus of my business have also discovered innovative new ways of working. For example, the software development team at Redstone Federal Credit Union in Huntsville, Alabama, shares its internally developed software solutions with other financial institutions worldwide using Open Solutions' unique online marketplace, the DNAappstore. In doing so, Redstone has turned its internal development team into a profit center rather than a G&A expense, and is leading the way in advancing collaboration among a global network of banks and credit unions.

Even the average consumer has begun taking steps to achieve a more sustainable American Dream. Since the post-financial crisis recession, Americans have been saving more and spending less. We are taking on less new debt and paying down the debt we have. Rather than being conspicuous consumers, we have become savvy shoppers, using price-comparison engines, online coupons, social buying networks and bidding sites – like ScoreBig and Priceline – to save money. While personal saving may not be boosting the economy in the short term, it is instilling prudent habits that will serve consumers well in the future.

It's easy to point out what's wrong with America, or with the world for that matter. What's not so easy is to change the way things are, to commit oneself to making things better – one person, one business or one community at a time. Theodore Roosevelt noted this important difference in his now-famous speech when he said:

> *It is not the critic who counts; not the man who points out how the strong man stumbles, or where the doer of deeds could have done them better. The credit belongs to the man who*

is actually in the arena, whose face is marred by dust and sweat and blood; who strives valiantly; who errs, who comes short again and again, because there is no effort without error and shortcoming; but who does actually strive to do the deeds; who knows great enthusiasms, the great devotions; who spends himself in a worthy cause; who at the best knows in the end the triumph of high achievement, and who at the worst, if he fails, at least fails while daring greatly, so that his place shall never be with those cold and timid souls who neither know victory nor defeat.[152]

We cannot afford to lose hope in the American Dream. It is what pulled us together as a country for nearly 250 years and made us one of the greatest nations in the history of the world. By the same token, we cannot afford to be complacent about the progress we have achieved. As any sports champion or business leader will attest, the most challenging task is not making it to the top of your field, it's staying there in the face of constant and ambitious competition.

America has always set its sights on doing great things. The time has now come for individuals and communities to be the "doers of deeds," leading the way forward to renew the promise of the American Dream.

If you think back to the time when you were a kid, you may have fantasized about being the one who caught the ball with 4 seconds on the clock to win the Super Bowl, or an ice skater whose final figure was a flawless triple toe loop that earned a perfect score from the judges, or the bold hero who rescued whomever it was you had a crush on at the time. It was all about being in the right place, at the right time, to make a difference.

---

[152] Theodore Roosevelt, "Citizenship in a Republic," Speech at the Sorbonne, Paris, France, April 23, 1910.

Today, America is facing one of the biggest social and economic dilemmas we have ever faced. We may talk about it with our neighbors at cocktail parties or with our business associates at work. But unlike other topics of discussion – whether it's the tsunami in Japan or the AIDS epidemic, where we have only a limited influence on the outcome – each of us has a very direct impact on the future stability and growth of our economy. It is important that we all, individually and collectively, take advantage of this opportunity to make a difference. It may be the single most important social contribution we will ever make. Today, we are all in the right place, at the right time, to make the difference we could only dream about as children. But we are no longer children; it's time to act and make our dream come true.

A Community on Board with the Dream...

I was a little girl when my parents decided to leave the beautiful island of Puerto Rico in 1990 and come to the United States. Even though Puerto Rico is a U.S. Commonwealth, my father believed I would find real opportunity only if we came to mainland America. What my father may never have imagined is the strength of my dream, and how it would help so many people living in my adopted home, a distressed city in Massachusetts.

My older siblings had already come to America when I arrived. I began attending middle school, and that's when my dream began to flicker. I saw the potential of my new home, the possibility of unlimited achievement. Even as a teenager, I believed in the value of hard work and dedication. There's much you can do in life. I didn't want to sit behind a desk or work for someone else. I wanted to own a business, and my family believed in me, saying, "You're the youngest one here; you can do better than all of us."

(continued on next page)

After I graduated from high school, I earned a degree in office administration at a local community college. Clerical jobs provided paychecks for several years, until the flicker turned into a flame. I opened a small transportation business in 2006. I bought two vans, hired two part-time drivers and they began shuttling children each morning to day care, school, after school programs and back home again at the end of the day.

Some people risk it all to achieve their dream. I was more cautious. I held onto my full-time job as an office clerk because I had a one-year-old son. I literally couldn't afford to fail. I worked full-time during the day and grew the business out of my home at night.

There were times when I feared failure – when gas prices rose and my budget became tight; when the economy sank and clients couldn't pay; when money was tight and I was afraid I'd have to close down. But a friend inspired me to pursue my dream, saying "There's somebody up there that's watching you, and you're doing a great job. Don't give up. You're doing a good thing for the community."

For the community? I had never thought about how much my small business was helping others who had their own goals, who also wanted to improve their lives. I had simply started a business with my own cash, financing from my family and, later on, a small business loan from a community bank.

Through word of mouth, the business grew to 13 vans and drivers transporting 228 children each week. My dream had come true, and with it, I was helping to fulfill a community of dreams.

(continued on next page)

When we pick up children, parents can work or attend school; they don't have to go in late or leave early because their children are on a different schedule; they don't have to worry about not having a car; they don't have to worry whether their children are in a safe place. They can focus on the task at hand. They can work toward achieving their dreams. Their children are ok, and I'll bring them home when their parents are ready. I never dreamed I'd be able to help so many people.

Milagros Brathwaite, President
Brathwaite Transportation, Inc.; Springfield, MA

CPSIA information can be obtained at www.ICGtesting.com
Printed in the USA
BVOW071909010512

289049BV00001B/2/P